Heal Yourself Then Heal Your Neighbor

A Five-Step Approach to Emotional Healing

SHARON L. MILLER, PH.D., LMHC
REV. GORDON S. MILLER, M.A.R. TH.

Based on Paraklasis Counseling Theory

Copyright© 2016 by Sharon Miller

ISBN- 13: 978-0692684368

All rights reserved.

First printed this edition 2016

HERITAGE INK PUBLISHING

Contents

Preface 5

Introduction: Loss—the Killer in the Shadows..........................7

PART ONE – HEAL YOURSELF
STEPS:
1 Identifying the Loss in Your Life...11
2 Identifying Substitutes—Phony or Real?...50
3 Replacing the Substitutes with the Truth.......................................59
4 Dealing with Future Loss God's Way..98
5 Loving Your Neighbor as Yourself...101

PART TWO – HEAL YOUR NEIGHBOR
STEPS:
1 Helping Your Neighbor Identify Loss...105
2 Helping Your Neighbor Identify Substitutes.....................................108
3 Helping Your Neighbor Replace Substitutes with Truth...........................111
4 Helping Your Neighbor Deal with Future Loss God's Way.........................119
5 Helping Your Neighbor Love His Neighbor as Himself............................124

Receiving and Giving Wise Counsel..129

Scripture Support for Helping Your Neighbor..131

Addendum...134

Conclusion...137

TO GOD BE THE GLORY GREAT THINGS HE HATH DONE!

Dr. Sharon Miller is a conference speaker, author, pastor, church planter, Licensed Mental Health Counselor (LMHC) and a Licensed Clinical Christian Therapist (LCCT), and online professor of Christian Life Coaching. Rev. Gordon Miller is an author, church planter, former U.S. Amy Chaplain, online theology professor, and pastor for forty years. They have been married for forty-eight years and have eleven adopted children.

PREFACE

After writing our book, *Paraklasis Counseling Theory* we realized that we had answered the need for a counseling theory that had biblical strength and scientific research behind it, but needed to answer the question, "Could it help anyone who needed emotional healing?" *Heal Yourself—Then Heal Your Neighbor* is a five-step approach to emotional healing that provides the answer to that question in a simplified approach to emotional healing that will enable the healed to bring healing to another hurting person. "Or how wilt thou say to thy brother, let me pull out the mote out of thine eye; and, behold, a beam is in thine own eye? Thou hypocrite, first cast out the beam out of thine own eye; and then shalt thou see clearly to cast out the mote out of thy brother's eye" (Matthew 7:4-5).

Hurt people, hurt people—and healed people, heal people. We have all suffered from loss and dealt with it in a variety of ways, some better than others. Loss creates emotional woundedness—a hurt that doesn't go away. As long as you hold the wounds in darkness they will never fully heal. Since we have all graduated from the university of suffering we should be considered experts in feeling upset, and at times overwhelmed with loss in one form or another. This book will help shine a light into those dark places in your life, and enable you to be changed from being a hurt person to a healed person, who can turn around and heal your neighbor.

INTRODUCTION

Loss – the killer in the shadows

Have you ever walked down a dark city street, late at night, when there are few people about? You hear your own footsteps more than any other sound. You experience hyper-vigilance, slight anxiety, and find your eyes looking behind you—finding that every shadow heightens your senses in a way that you don't feel when the light approaches. You should feel the same way about undiscovered loss in your life. Much counseling focuses on the symptoms of anger, anxiety, depression, and so on, without realizing that loss is the killer of living life to its fullest. It often remains hiding in the shadows of our minds, lurking with sinister intent, looking for the ideal time to strike with devastating consequences, and then retreating to the shadows once again, rarely discovered for what it is, and has potential to do. Loss has diabolical plans to rob and kill, and then disguise itself as an angel of light bringing deceit and substitutes for the loss that has occurred, thus multiplying itself and creating more loss. Loss has its origins in the one who brought it about—the Serpent, who deceived Adam and Eve, bringing it upon every man, woman, and child who has ever lived.

How easy it is to not see the lies that support our substitutes because they are so deeply hidden behind the truth of our emotional pain. It isn't until we look behind our emotional pain into the loss that was experienced that we are able to see clearly the lie we believed. You can't find lies standing next to the truth; they are always hiding behind the truth.

Perception is the way we look at things. My perception of what is in good taste in clothing preferences may differ from someone else's choices. My perception of what is a great looking automobile may differ completely from another person. These are just two simple examples of how perception is very personal and influences our choices. When it comes to various events in life that bring loss, perception is critical for a counselor because one person's perception of an event is different from another's perception. What may be considered terrible, catastrophic loss may mean nothing to the person going through the life-changing event. An example would be of the man who lost his wife suddenly in a car accident. His family sends him to a counselor who is ready to give him crisis counseling, but is puzzled by the lack of loss going through his mind. When the truth comes out, it is discovered that the woman had a huge life insurance policy, and the man had a woman on the side and was planning on a divorce. His perception of catastrophic loss was that it was nothing significant. Perception of the loss is a major player in the amount of emotional pain that one experiences.

PART ONE

HEAL YOURSELF

STEP ONE
Identifying the Loss in Your Life

Midway on our life's journey, I found myself
In dark woods, the right road lost. To tell
About those woods is hard – so tangled and rough
And savage that thinking of it now, I feel
The old fear stirring: death is hardly more bitter.
-The Inferno of Dante, Canto I

"Search me, O God, and know my heart; try me, and know my anxieties; and see if there is any wicked way in me, and lead me in the way everlasting" (Psalm 139:23-24, NKJ).

"Examine me, O LORD, and prove me; try my mind and my heart" (Psalm 26:2, NKJ).

"Search me, O God, and know my heart; Try me, and know my anxieties; And see if *there is any* wicked way in me, and lead me in the way everlasting" (Psalm 139:23-24).

"For there is not a word in my tongue, but, lo, O LORD, thou knowest it altogether. Thou hast beset me behind and before, and laid thine hand upon me" (2 Corinthians 13:5).

"Come unto me, all ye that labour and are heavy laden, and I will give you rest" (Matthew 11:28).

"He healeth the broken in heart, and bindeth up their wounds" (Psalm 147:3).

Loss comes and loss goes, like people who enter your kitchen with dirty shoes. You forget exactly who it was, or when it was, but the dirt is the only thing left on the floor. Loss leaves its dirty footprint long after we forget how it walked into our lives. Sometimes all the details of loss that came to us a long time ago are foggy in our memories, but the dirt remains in our day to day lives. The effect of that loss still hurts us, and we are often not even aware of it because as Dante said, "…To tell about those dark woods is hard—so tangled and rough…"

In order to identify the loss, perception of that loss must be understood. The ancient Hindu story of the six blind men and the elephant is relevant in understanding how loss can be perceived differently, depending on where you stand and what part of loss you are feeling. The story is about six blind men in a small village who heard people shouting that there was an elephant walking through the village. The blind men had never seen an elephant, so they had no idea what an elephant was. They decided that they needed to feel the elephant. They all began touching the elephant and describing to each other what they were feeling. The first man said that the elephant was like a tree because he touched its leg. The second man said the elephant was like a rope as he grabbed its tail. The third man touched the elephant's trunk and said it was like a branch of a tree. The fourth man touched the ear and said it was like a big hand fan. The fifth man touched its belly and said that was like a huge wall. The sixth man said that it was like a smooth pipe, as he touched the elephant's tusk. All six men began to argue about the elephant, each insisting that what he thought was correct and was truly the elephant. A wise man was passing by, and stopped to intervene. He asked them what the problem was, and each man explained their different experiences. The wise man told them they were all right, but that they all perceived it differently because each man touched a different part of the elephant. The elephant had all of those characteristics. The dispute was resolved, and all six blind men were happy because they were all right.

When it comes to loss, just like any object, or idea, while people may see or feel things differently, they can still all be right. Different aspects of that life-changing event may be more or less important to some people than others. The temptation for someone who is trying to bring help to someone who has experienced loss is to help them through their own perception of that loss, which really means that we are like the six blind men. What is necessary is to discover how the person perceives that loss, not how we perceive it.

Identifying your own loss involves looking at the totality of your life. Usually loss is identified by the major life-changing events in your life. We all suffer loss from the time we leave the womb and the quiet comfort of that safe place. However, loss that leaves painful reminders that it was there, and affects us with issues in our lives is what is to be examined, since present psychological pain comes from loss.

Loss that is occurring in present time is called aleph loss. Loss that happened in the past is called tav loss. Aleph loss can become tav loss, and tav loss can become aleph loss. For example, a painful past experience can cause emotional distress in the present, such as sexual child abuse, or combat PTSD. The past loss, or tav loss, becomes aleph loss, in the present. On the other hand, present loss, or aleph loss, can become tav loss (past loss) in the process of counseling. What happens at this point is that your past loss is no longer creating issues and pain in the present. Recognizing aleph (present loss) and tav loss (past loss) enables the one to understand how intense the loss was, or how it was perceived by the person who suffered the loss. Understanding these two sub-categories of loss will help you assess the loss in your own life and how it has been perceived by you.

In order to identify the loss in your own life, look at the loss events in your life and find the category—one or more—that fits from the Nine Categories of Secondary Loss listed below. Remember that primary loss is the loss of relationship with God as a result of a person not knowing Jesus Christ as their Savior and Lord. Secondary Loss is the loss experienced, whether Christian or non-Christian, by living in this world.

If you are a Christian, then you will be writing down the significant secondary loss events in your life. These are events that have diminished your security, safety, or significance (sometimes all three). For example, one of your parents committed suicide when you were a child, or, your parents divorced when you were a child, or perhaps you experienced the loss of a job that left you in financial trouble. Maybe you went through a divorce yourself. An accident that disfigured you, or loss of a limb from combat, or, the combat experience that left you with PTSD, illness, a traumatic experience, grief, rape, abuse, a near-death experience, are just some examples of things that create loss in our lives.

As you pray and ask the Lord to bring to mind some of these losses, you may be surprised at events in your life that you did not even consider losses until God brought them to your mind. At this step, you are not trying to solve anything, but to become aware of your own perception of these life events. Writing them down is very important.

We recommend that you don't rush the process of your emotional healing. Find a quiet place, free of distractions, and invite God to release His healing power into your life. The following is a simple prayer that you may want use to allow Him to release His healing into your damaged and wounded emotions. "He healeth the broken in heart, and bindeth up their wounds" (Psalm 147:3).

Father, you say in your Word that You are the healer of the brokenhearted and that You will heal my emotional wounds. Give me the strength I need to face the wounds of the past and to understand the loss that I have experienced that has left an opening in my heart and life. Show me, by the power of Your Holy Spirit how I have allowed negative attitudes and behaviors in my life to rob me of true significance, true safety, and true security. Help me to sense your love and presence in a deeper way than ever before, in Jesus' name, Amen.

IDENTIFYING THE LOSS BY EXAMINING THE THE NINE CATEGORIES OF SECONDARY LOSS

Category I

Loss Caused by Another's Sinful Choice

Genesis 37; 39-45—Joseph
1 Peter 2:19-23; John 15:18-20—Jesus
2 Corinthians 11:23-26—Paul
2 Timothy 3:10-12—All who live a godly life in Christ

Genesis 4 describes the first murder in mankind by Cain killing his brother Abel. Although it is not recorded for us, Adam and Eve experienced the first time man grieved over the loss of a son. Adam and Eve both experienced Category I, Loss Caused by Another's Sinful Choice. Just knowing that murder was possible because of what they had done in disobeying God could have affected their safety, security, and significance.

An example of Category I Loss would be the person who steals from another. You experience loss of what the thief stole. The devil is an expert at stealing our safety, security, and significance. Christians must be on guard against him. What distinguishes this category from other categories is that it is a deliberate, premeditated, sinful choice. In the Bible, David stole Bathsheba from her husband and then took his life.

Some persons who have received Category I Loss from Another's Sinful Choice have been the victims of those who took away their reputations, money, and even their chastity. In your experience, this loss may be something that humiliated you, or brought hurt to you in some way. It came about as a sinful decision on someone's part that affected your safety, security, or significance. Abuse, verbal, physical, or sexual, as a child or an adult would be one example. A divorce brought about by your spouse's unfaithfulness is another example. These are just examples and not in any way all inclusive.

- The hurt I experienced:

It affected me by:

- The hurt I experienced:

It affected me by:

Category II

Loss Caused by Your Own Sinful Choice

Judges 13: 1-16:31—Samson
1 Samuel 16:1-11; 2 Samuel 12; 2 Samuel 24:25—David

II Samuel 12 narrates how David's sin of taking Uriah the Hittite's wife to be his own, and having Uriah to be murdered, is exposed by God through Nathan the prophet. As a result of those two sins David will never have murderous violence leave his family line. There will be a loss of peace in his family. God will also raise up one who would take David's wives from him and defile them. What David did secretly, God will cause to happen openly. Also, his child, born of that sin will die because David's sinful choice made the enemies of God to blaspheme. David experienced Category II, Loss Caused by Your Own Sinful Choice. David went through living with his family in ruins, because he destroyed another's family. Even though the loss was terrible, David was told that his sins were forgiven, that he would not die.

An example of this category is when you have made decisions in your life that were clearly in opposition to God's Word, the Bible. As a result, you have made sinful choices and suffered loss. You perhaps lost your good health because of drinking and taking drugs. Or, you are a Christian and you married an unbeliever who deserted you, or became unfaithful, and you have suffered the loss of a good marriage. Some people make the sinful choice of robbing and stealing or breaking the law in some way and suffered the loss of their freedom in their incarceration, or even probation. (List the decisions that God brings to your mind that were in opposition to His Word and the loss it caused.)

- The choice I made that was in opposition to His Word was:

The loss this choice caused in my life:

- The choice I made that was in opposition to His Word was:

The loss this choice caused in my life:

Category III

Loss from Living in a Sin-Cursed World

John 11:1-44—Lazarus

Genesis 47:13-27—Famine in the land

John 21—No fish

Immediately after the primary loss of losing relationship with God because of Adam's sin, God judged the serpent that tempted them to sin by promising eternal death to him through the seed of the woman, Jesus Christ, and enmity between the serpent's seed and the woman's seed. In other words, the serpent having brought ruination on mankind and the earth, could not have it his way all the time. There would be part of humanity that would oppose his will due to enmity that God put between the two parts of mankind. The meaning of "dust shalt thou eat" is that the devil will live in continual disappointment in life.

In 2001 a research study on universal loss, by Judith Murray, three fundamental assumptions held by people in Western cultures are identified. First, the world is benevolent. Second, the world is just and meaningful, and third, the self is worthy. Therefore, if a person is good, then major loss can be avoided. When major loss occurs then life is no longer meaningful or controllable and these beliefs may be abandoned. When the loss comes and the beliefs are rigidly held, then people may make harsh moral judgments about themselves and others.

From a Christian biblical worldview, the world suffers from the curse of sin. Therefore, just and benevolent is not necessarily the best terms to describe it. The self, whether regenerated or not, is not worthy, other than being in God's image and is in need of a heart change that the Bible calls regeneration. The self is saved by grace, not by worth. Grace is a gift, not something earned.

As Christians are God's children they are loved by Him, but still suffer from a sin-cursed world that God permits. For example, people lose their jobs, Christians get terminal diseases, fruit trees die from disease before they bear fruit, and buildings collapse and kill people. Tornadoes, hurricanes and tsunamis take their toll of human and animal life. Famines kill crops and people. The rain falls on the fields to water the crops of the just and the unjust. Good things even happen to bad people. In His plan of redemption, the curse of sin and its effects on man's environment will only end when the Lord Jesus returns to create a new world, without the curse of sin and death. Life in this world is topsy-turvy, not very predictable.

Therefore, since the world is less predictable, loss has a tendency to make people more fearful. There is a need to rebuild a sense of safety, security, and significance in the midst of a changing environment. A

Christian, biblical worldview should be taught by the Church. It would help Christians in crisis mode from the damage done by sudden, catastrophic loss.

This category of secondary loss has probably caused more loss than any other category. It affects all Christians in some form. The loss of good health because of illness, or the loss of the use of limbs from military combat, or an auto accident; the loss of freedom due to aging. There are many different examples for this category of loss. The loss of the price of selling a house because the economy has declined is another example.

Loss seldom exists alone. It is often accompanied by other resultant losses. Loss multiplies loss. For example, there may be a disability as the result of the loss of good health. As a result, there may be a loss of independence and mobility, and as a result, there may very likely be a loss of finances which may lead to loss in significance, safety and security if a person does not have the inoculation from a Christian worldview.

A major loss can cause the multiplication of loss. A person may have a loss of safety from a rape, which may result in freedom of movement due to excessive fear. (Carefully examine your life for loss caused by living in a sin-cursed world and describe the loss and how it affected you.

- The loss I experienced from living in a sin-cursed world:

- The way it affected me or changed my life:

Category IV

Voluntary Loss for Secondary Gain

1 Samuel 24—David loses kingship for righteousness' sake to gain the kingship God's way

John 16:21—Temporary sorrow leading to joy

College students often suffer this loss. They lose money and the ability to live independently by not working with the secondary gain of getting a college degree. A single parent loses the extra time and rest by working two jobs for the secondary gain of providing for the needs of his/her children. Perhaps the choice to leave college and start a family might bring loss of one's plans for the future for the secondary gain of starting a family. A person may decide not to fix their car so they have more money to spend on other things, or to sacrifice getting a newer car for obtaining a college education. It is similar to the game of chess, where you sacrifice a pawn to get a queen.

    Comfort from this category of loss can come from the fact that God promises us a future and a hope in the Word of God. God promised David that he would be the king of Israel, but he voluntarily passed by the opportunity of killing King Saul to reach that goal God's way and not man's way. He suffered voluntary loss for secondary gain.

What is interesting is that he didn't suffer emotionally because his decision was a righteous decision, according to Scripture.

God also promises to give us the desires of our hearts. Some of these desires need to be reevaluated in light of more important ones. As Christians, walking by faith, and not by sight pleases God. We may have to put off obtaining some of the desires, develop trust in God, and learn patience, as time passes by. All of these things will occur in God's plan, which is always better than our best idea. (List any losses you may have experienced that were for secondary gain.)

- The loss I experienced so I could gain something else was:

- This choice affected my life by:

Category V

Voluntary Loss for Christ

Philippians 1:12-26—Paul's imprisonment for the Gospel

Philippians 3:7,8—Paul's gain in knowing Christ.

Christian missionaries lose living with an abundance of money and all the benefits of living in their home country, facing the loss of safety by going to another country for the secondary gain of getting rewards in Heaven, and seeing people come to know Jesus Christ as their Savior. Christians that follow God's leading, walking in His will, often experience this category of loss. Jesus tells us about the potential loss for serving Him when He warns that sometimes even our families will turn against us for putting Christ first. In Iraq, Christians are being persecuted, even crucified, for refusing to bow the knee to Islam.

John and Betty Stam were missionaries with China Inland Mission. They were described as a young couple filled with the love of Christ. On December 6. 1934, the Red forces captured the city of Tsingteh, China. Betty was bathing her little daughter, Helen, born less than three months earlier on September 11. As John and Betty kneeled down to pray, a loud knocking was heard on their door. John opened the door, and while he was trying to satisfy the leaders demands for money and other items, Betty was serving them something to eat. Kindness was not enough for the intruders. John was bound and taken away to the Communist headquarters, and eventually they returned for the new mom and her baby.

They were both bound with tight ropes with their hands behind them. Stripped of all of their outer clothing they passed down the street amidst shouting ridicule and invitations to view their execution. John was asked to kneel. There was joy on his face as he was ordered to kneel and then his spirit was released. His wife fell to her knees beside him and in a flash of a sword, they were reunited. The baby, Helen, had been left in a deserted house, lying on the bed, just as her dear mother's hands had left her, was rescued and brought to safety. What an example of voluntary loss for Christ.

Philippians 3:7,8 reveals Paul's perception and subjective value of his loss. Loss itself is something that has been perceived as valuable that is now gone. Paul was willing to forego his security, safety and significance in Judaism for knowing Christ because Paul knew that these three basic needs are fully met in knowing Jesus Christ. (If this applies to you then list those voluntary losses.)

- What I voluntarily gave up to serve God:

- This affected my life by:

- Read the following verses and record your thoughts.

Phil. 1:21:

Phil. 3:7-8:

Matthew 19:21:

Mark 8:35:

Mark 9:35:

John 12:24:

Hebrews 11:24-27:

Category VI

Loss of a Loved One

John 11—Mary and Martha's loss of Lazarus

John 19—Loss at Jesus' crucifixion

John 11:35—"Jesus wept"

Isaiah 53:3—Jesus acquainted with grief

1 Thessalonians 4:13-14; 2 Samuel 12:20-23—Hope of reuniting

2 Corinthians 1:3-5—Comfort

"When the perishable puts on the imperishable, and the mortal puts on immortality, then shall come to pass the saying that it is written: 'Death is swallowed up in victory. O death, where is your victory? O death, where is your sting?' The sting of death is sin, and the power of sin is the law. But thanks be to God, who gives us the victory through our Lord Jesus Christ"

(1 Corinthians 15:54-55)

People lose loved ones through death. Everyone must deal with loss by death at some point in their lives. Death came as a result of the Fall. Death is regarded as an enemy and the last enemy that will be cast into the lake of fire. Death causes a tearing apart of relationships among people, and bereavement varies in length of time.

Grief from loss of a loved one doesn't follow a linear pattern. You don't go through the process of grief as though it was a clear path that begins at the loss and then you move straight through anger, sadness, etc. until you come to the end of your grieving. Just when you think you have reached the end, it starts all over again and you find yourself dealing with the same stages you thought you had already gone through successfully, perhaps skipping a stage that you have already made progress in as you move along through the process of healing. Not everyone going through grief will experience anger and the rest of the stages of grief. Everyone is a unique individual working through their unique circumstances.

No matter how you go through the grieving process, the goal is to continue to move through the process and eventually move out without any self-destructive behaviors that may arise from denial, despair, loneliness, bitterness, or unforgiveness. God promises in His Word that he will be with us even though we walk through the valley of the shadow of death (Psalm 23). We have the promise that He cares for us (1 Peter 5:6-7).

Resist the temptation to be angry at God. Deep within us we realize that death is unnatural and our deepest soul desire is to cry out for justice and find a way to put an end to the devastation that it causes in our own lives and the lives of others. Be careful that your anger at death doesn't become misdirected toward God or others. Remember that the God you serve never sins, and He is just. Don't direct your anger at God or friends, but instead at the enemy—sin. "The anger of man does not produce the righteousness of God" (James 1:20).

Death comes in so many unexpected ways. We might be caught off guard by an unexpected loss, but it didn't catch God off guard. "Are not two sparrows sold for a penny? And not one of them will fall to the ground apart from your Father. But even the hairs on your head are all numbered. Fear not, therefore; you are of more value than many sparrows" (Matthew 10:29-31).

One of the most important themes in the literature on bereavement is continuing the bond between the living and the dead. Some degree of attachment is normal, but sometimes it can be maladaptive. It is difficult for one who loses a loved one when they cannot make sense of the loss. One possible reason is that the situation may be influenced by the person's own fears of death. When there is a strong Christian worldview, there is at least the element of faith that straightens people in the uncertainty of why a loved one dies. This lessens the pain that people go through when nothing makes any sense.

- My loss was:

- How I grieved:

- Problems it created:

There is no right or wrong way to grieve because everyone grieves differently, but as a believer, you can turn to God's Word for your strength and comfort during the grieving process. Read each of the following verses and mark the ones that give you comfort in your situation. Write those verses down and keep them where you can refer to them.

Matthews 5:4	2 Corinthians 1:3-4
Isaiah 41:10	Isaiah 43:2
Psalm 18:28	Psalm 46:1-2
Revelation 21:4	Psalm 119:50
Romans 8:18	1 Thessalonians 4:13-18
Peter 5:6-7	Psalm 23:4
Psalm 73:26	Psalm 22:24
Psalm 27:4-5	Psalm 30:5
Psalm 34:18	Matthew 11:28
Lamentations 3:31-33	Romans 8:31-39
Corinthians 15:52-57	1 Peter 1:3-9
1 John 14:1-4	

Every step of the process of grieving is natural and it is healthy. The only time that it can become unhealthy and destructive, and even dangerous, is when the person grieving gets stuck in one step of grieving for a long time. The ultimate goal of grieving is not that all pain or all memories of the loss is eliminated, but true recovery is the stage where you will begin to show renewed interest in your daily activities and start to live each day in a normal way. This requires the time to reorganize your life and move the loss from the center of your life to a place that is still an important part of your life. The verses listed above will help you reach your goal of moving ahead and living your life to the Glory of God.

Category VII

Loss Caused by the Actions of Another

Luke 2:1-7—Mary the mother of Jesus

Genesis 4:2-7—Cain's loss of significance leads to jealousy and murder.

Acts 27—Paul is affected by the centurion's decision to ignore Paul's advice.

This loss is not caused by someone sinning against another, but an example may be that a company must downsize and someone loses their job. The actions of another may not be personal at all, but nevertheless, the actions of someone else, results in a loss event for another. An injury in an automobile accident due to a defect in the automobile's breaking system is an example of this category of loss.

Loss by the actions of another can lead people to fatal aggression. How many people have murdered people they do not even know in mass murders at movie theaters or malls that have their roots in this category of loss caused by the actions of another? Loss in this category may not be as severe as described above, but the principle that loss multiplies loss suggests a simmering build-up of an angry response that could reach the "breaking point" if not dealt with, or cause significant behavior problems. Unfortunately, in contemporary therapy, this way of looking at loss has been overlooked.

This category of loss can hurt us in less obvious ways than the extreme cases of murder or jealousy. The actions of another may have caused someone to feel neglected, forgotten, not valued, insignificant, ignored, insecure, jealous, angry, depressed, frustrated, etc. Actions caused by another may have halted your dreams, your plans, your future, and can even destroy the desire to live. The actions of another may very well come from someone who does not even know they are causing such pain and devastation.

In Acts 27 we see a good example of loss caused by the actions of another. Paul was going on a ship to Rome as a prisoner who was to appear before Caesar. During the voyage, Paul advised that the trip will end with disaster and much loss of cargo, the ship, and lives. The person who could make the decision to take another route was the centurion who as commanding the ship. Although Paul knew the outcome, the only thing he could do was advise, and the centurion took the advice of the owner of the ship and made the opposite decision.

Perhaps in regard to this category of loss, something was out of your hands, and just as Paul, you couldn't jump ship. Sometimes we can get ourselves out of a dangerous decision that others may make, and as Paul, sometimes we can't. An example is that we can't jump out of our family just because someone in the family has made a wrong decision in his or her life, and those decisions bring loss into our lives as well.

As a result of another's decision, the ship eventually lost cargo, was tempest tossed, and it appeared that lives would be lost, but Paul stood up and spoke and informed them that although they lost cargo and ship, that no lives would be lost because Paul could announce that "for there stood by me this night an angel of the God to whom I belong and whom I serve, saying, 'Do not be afraid Paul; you must be brought before Caesar; and indeed God has granted you all those who sail with you.' Therefore, take heart, men, for I believe God that it will be just as it was told me. However, we must run aground on a certain island" (Acts 27:15-26). Even though Paul told them not to do so, this didn't exclude Paul and the other believers from experiencing the loss that came about from the actions of another.

Read the following Scriptures for examples of loss caused by the actions of another.

(1 Samuel 20) Jonathan suffers the loss of his friend best friend, David, due to the actions of his father.

(Jonah 1) The sailors on the ship that took Jonah to Tarshish suffered the trauma of going through a terrible storm because of Jonah's refusal to go to Nineveh.

(Numbers 14) Joshua and Caleb experience loss when they do not get to enter the Promised Land for forty years because of the Israelites' disobedience.

(Luke 22:48) Jesus' suffering began with the betrayal by Judas.

- The loss I experienced due to someone else's actions was:

- This loss caused me to:

Category VIII

Loss Caused by Your Own Choice (Not Sinful)

Genesis 13; Genesis 19—Lot's choice of land and the result
Matthew 25:14-30—The talents

A man takes a loan to open a restaurant, the fulfillment of his dreams. Everyone in the small town knows this person, but within two years the business fails. The owner has lost significance, and feels like a failure. Now he has lost employment and his life savings and his home is in foreclosure. He has lost security and safety. This is an example of loss caused by your own choice, not necessarily sinful. We all make choices that sometimes cause us suffering and problems in life, and some of these choices cause loss in an area of life due to those choices.

    At times when our backs are against the wall due to loss caused by a choice we made it is time to be completely dependent upon God. He instructs us to call on Him for help. "...and call on me in the day of trouble; I will deliver you, and you will honor me" (Psalm 50:15). A loss in this category can make it seem like everything is closing in on us, and our hope is dashed so that we become completely hopeless. This hopelessness can lead to despair and then to depression.

Another way that this category of loss can affect us is through anxiety that is created by the circumstances that it caused. Anxiety attacks may last just for a few minutes, or for days, sometimes creating a continuous cycle of attack after attack, and just when you think you have it under control something comes along and triggers it all over again. The loss that this category can create brings fear for the present and the future, and these fears demand attention and if not checked will continue to demand more and more.

High in the Rocky Mountains in Colorado there is a point that is along the Continental Divide where there is a topographic feature that causes a small stream to separate and some of the water flows into the Colorado River, and eventually into the Gulf of California and then into the Pacific Ocean. Some of the water will flow into the Mississippi River and eventually into the Gulf of Mexico and then the Atlantic Ocean. So as the rain falls, two drops of water can wind up in the complete opposite direction. Choices we make are a bit like the drops of rain that fall into that stream. The choice may not seem very significant at the time, but it sets a chain reaction of events that move and flow and change our lives and many around us, sometimes for generations. Some of our choices will not be good, and bring about bad consequences, and other choices we make may be good choices, but we may still suffer some loss as a result.

- My own choices that caused me problems:

- What I lost due to my choice was:

Category IX

Loss Caused by Someone in Authority

Luke 15:28—Story of the Prodigal Son

This is a recently discovered category of loss with some overlap with loss caused by another, or loss caused by another's sin. The wrong use of authority or the perception that someone misused their authority, causing a loss of safety, security, or significance is strong enough to become a separate category. Children who have been abused by someone they should have been able to trust, like parents, or step-parents, an adult, someone in ministry, a teacher, or a coach have been affected deeply by that betrayal. Sometimes there is the perception of a neglect of authority; in other words, a child may feel that the parent failed to protect them from those who hurt them, or didn't love them as they needed. An example is in the parable of the Prodigal Son, where the elder brother perceived neglect, and experienced loss from this category of loss caused by someone in authority.

The loss of significance, safety, and security caused by this category are worked out in dysfunctional substitutes, such as seeking authority in a gang, or evidenced by a child placed in a loving foster family who then becomes defiant and exhibits resistive behavior. This behavior becomes a substitute for lack of trust. People who have continually perceived to be unfairly treated by a supervisor in the United States Post Office, have reacted in violent ways, popularly called "going postal." This is another example. This is what causes people to rebel against governments. Rebellion against authority is the substitute that man often chooses.

The OT and the NT have these examples. David trusted King Saul at first, and then Saul attempted to murder him, and as he fled for many years from cave to cave in the wilderness, he suffered from Category Nine, Loss from Someone in Authority. David was considered Public Enemy Number One in his nation. This was an incredible loss of significance, safety, and security. Only his faith in God, internalizing his beliefs, gave him the inner strength to righteously respond, and not seek unrighteous substitutes for the loss.

The story in the parable of the prodigal son is a familiar one to most people. In Luke 15:28, the statement regarding the elder brother is revealing, "And he was angry, and would not go in..." This is another example of Category Nine Loss, Loss from Someone in Authority. His father was in authority. He was hosting a party for the rebellious son who came home. The elder brother had never been rebellious, and the father never threw him a party to show his love for him.

He suffered a loss of significance from Category Nine Loss. His father did love him, but his perception was that he loved the rebel far more than the faithful son. Perception controls our response to life's situations, making them better than they are, or worse than they are.

- Person or persons that have treated me unfairly are:

- Their abuse, neglect, or unfair treatment has caused me to feel:

- Ways that I have rebelled against authority as a result of the above:

- I lost the following as a result:(Check the appropriate box or boxes.)

    o   Safety
    o   Security
    o   Significance

STEP TWO

Identifying Substitutes, Phony or Real

> Then, a grim she-wolf-whose leanness seemed to compress
> All the world's craving that had made miserable
> Such multitudes; she put such heaviness
> Into my spirit, I lost hope of the crest.
> Like someone eager to win, who tested by loss
> Surrenders to gloom and weeps, so did that beast
> Make me feel, as harrying toward me at a lope
> She forced me back toward where the sun is lost.
>
> -The Inferno of Dante, Canto I

It is built into human nature to seek a substitute for what was lost. It is the reason teenage boys who have no father living in the home seek a father image in gangs. It is why aging and famous actresses get plastic surgery. It is also why the gambler who loses all his money at the casino sells his Rolex watch for fifty dollars, so that he can try to win back what he has lost. There is always the insatiable desire to replace what is lost, with something, sometimes anything, whether it is good for a person or not. We call those things substitutes for loss. The Bible tells us that after the Fall, man found a substitute for God by worshiping the creature, rather than the Creator. That is a substitute for Primary Loss.

There are substitutes also for Secondary Loss, which consists of all types of loss that happens apart from not knowing God. Some substitutes are relatively harmless and do not cause emotional pain, like losing your wedding ring and buying a cheaper substitute. In this case, the substitute may not be the same as the original, which was lost, but still serves the purpose. It is a harmless substitute.

A recent television drama showed a man whose wife was dying of cancer. He had a hard time even being with her while she was dying. He tried to get away from the pain by immersing himself in his work. One day, his desk drawer was stuck. He struggled more and more with opening it—all the time getting more and more angry. With a yell of anger that caused the other workers' heads to turn, he yanked it out with all his strength and it fell on the floor, sending its contents in all directions. He then looked around and left the room until he calmed down. While he was absent from the room the sympathetic co-workers picked up the contents of the drawer for him and put it back. This is another example of substitutes. The anger he expressed at the drawer was the anger he felt at the cancer, but was not able to express for obvious reasons. This is not a particularly harmful substitute, unless you are the desk drawer, but the man, when spoken to by a friend immediately after the incident, did not understand his feelings.

If he starts taking that anger out on other family members, friends, and children, he could benefit from counseling. Probably at least once in our lives, we have all been in this man's shoes. It is a natural thing to want to find a substitute to take out our anger, when it would be inappropriate to do it directly.

Other substitutes are not as harmless. There is a need for a replacement from the loss which is man's defense mechanism. There is a need of replacement when significance, safety, or security is lost. It can take the form of rationalization, compensation, denial, or harmful substitutes that may create an insatiable desire for more, as in hoarding. The principle that loss multiplies loss is true. For the Christian, some substitutes may be harmful and sinful, others may not be harmful, or sinful, but for the non-Christian, all substitutes are harmful because from God's viewpoint, whatever is not of faith, is sin, and it is idolatry: "…whatever is not from faith is sin" (Romans 14:23). It is always harmful to the person in primary loss (not knowing Jesus Christ as Savior) who seeks a substitute for God in the areas of significance, safety, or security.

Loss of significance means that you have no voice, nothing worthwhile to say, and no one would listen because you are not worth listening to anyway. The Greek word *aphonos*, found in Acts 8:32, means voiceless, without faculty of speech. To be voiceless means you have no significance whatsoever. This Scripture is a prophecy from the Old Testament, of Jesus as the sacrificial sin-offering "…He was led as a sheep to the slaughter; and like a lamb dumb before his shearer, so opened he not his mouth…" This was part of Jesus' humiliation as a sin-offering, meaning that He would not speak to defend Himself. The Lord Jesus, in the state of His humiliation transitioned three ways in His descent into Hell. He lost His freedom to actively move about, then lost His ability to speak to defend Himself, then He lost His ability to freely think. If He could have found any peace, while hanging on the cross, then He would not have experienced the full wrath of God.

The first sin of Adam began in the mind. Jesus was torn between being justly punished, and not justly punished. This was the divine paradox. Before He was ultimately condemned, He was within the gates and had a right of appeal to His Father in Heaven, in His mind. After He was condemned and taken out of the gates, He became accursed. His right of appeal to God was taken away. His refuge was gone. The Lord Himself opposed Him in His mind. He had no more voice. He had no more significance as a human being. He had to be absolutely miserable. Loss takes significance away.

Some people believe that they have significance, but it may be a false significance. False significance leads to little significance. Little significance leads to no significance. It is a downhill slide. Ecclesiastes 2:9-11 tells us that the king is great in his own eyes because he can enjoy all the pleasures of the world. He rejoices in his worldly occupation. When it did not satisfy, and loss was involved, it led to little significance. (Ecclesiastes 2:11) "…all is vanity." Eventually, it led to "…hating life" (v. 17)), which means no significance. Loss multiplies loss.

For the Old Testament Israelite, God's promise of safety was primarily from the enemies of Israel, from Egypt to the Canaanites and the Amalekites. The importance of the depth of safety in relation to the human soul will be seen as one reflects upon these verses. So, not only is physical safety involved, but spiritual and emotional safety as well. "Wherefore ye shall do my statutes, and keep my judgments, and do them; and ye shall dwell in the land in safety. And the land shall yield her fruit, and ye shall eat your fill, and dwell therein in safety" (Leviticus 25:18-19). Notice that obedience leads to fruitfulness, and that results in safety.

The Lord Jesus is our example of someone who lost all nine categories of loss, and lost His safety, security, and significance. Since the Lord Jesus is our example, and He survived without being driven to false, sinful substitutes, we can have hope that we can get through the worst loss without destructive emotional results. In the middle of His loss of earthly significance, safety, and security, He cared beyond Himself to provide security for His mother.

Sometimes the Lord taps the substitute on the shoulder and cuts into the dance of life just at the right time, changing the idolatrous dance into a dance of praise. "Thou hast turned for me my mourning into dancing: thou hast put off my sackcloth, and girded me with gladness" (Psalm 30:11).

Man can deal with loss when he finds his significance in Christ (Romans 6). Loss cannot remove significance, safety, and security when someone walks after the Spirit, and not the flesh. "There is therefore now no condemnation to them that are in Christ Jesus, who walk not after the flesh, but after the Spirit." The world, the flesh, and the devil are devalued by the intellect that is driven by a new heart and values Jesus above everything" (Romans 8:1). "But what things were gain to me, those I counted loss for Christ. Yea doubtless, and I count all things loss for the excellency of the knowledge of Christ Jesus my Lord: for whom I have suffered the loss of all things, and count them dung, that I may win Christ" (Philippians 3:7-8). As a result, the person is full of gratitude and praise. "But that on the good ground are they, which in an honest and good heart, having heard the word, keep it and bring forth fruit with patience" (Luke 8:15). "A new heart also will I give you, and a new spirit will I put within you: and I will take away the stony heart out of your flesh, and I will give you a heart of flesh" (Ezekiel 36:26).

Good psychological health discerns the true value of self and relationships when worthless substitutes are discarded and replaced by truth. This is not accomplished by human reasoning but only by the grace of God's intervention into a person's life.

If man does not have security, safety, or significance in Christ, substitutes are sought out in this lifetime dance of idolatry.) "Who changed the truth of God into a lie, and worshipped and served the creature more than the Creator, who is blessed forever" (Romans 1:25).

"For this ye know, that no whoremonger, nor unclean person, nor covetous man, who is an idolater, hath any inheritance in the kingdom of Christ and of God" (Ephesians 5:5).

Man is always looking for a better partner to dance the dance of life. The unfortunate man always finds death as his dancing partner. "But every man is tempted, when he is drawn away of his own lust, and enticed. Then when lust hath conceived, it bringeth forth sin: and sin, when it is finished, bringeth forth death" (James 1:14-15). None of the substitutes satisfy. "Now the doings (practices) of the flesh are clear (obvious); they are immorality, impurity, indecency, idolatry, sorcery, enmity, strife, jealousy, anger (ill temper), selfishness, divisions (dissensions), party spirit (factions, sects with peculiar opinions, heresies" (Galatians 5:19-21, Amplified Bible).

After trying them all, the worst predicament to be in, is to realize that loss is total and complete in life. "For if after they have escaped the pollutions of the world through the knowledge of the Lord and Savior Jesus Christ, they are again entangled therein, and overcome, the latter end is worse with them than the beginning. For it had been better for them not to have known the way of righteousness, than, after they have known it, to turn from the holy commandment delivered unto them. But it is happened unto them according to the true proverb, "The dog is turned to his own vomit again; and the sow that was washed to her wallowing in the mire" (2 Peter 2:20-22).

This may be the counselor's or people helper's opportunity to help the client to see that substitutes for God always fail. People are seldom in the complete awareness state of the triangle of Total Loss (Safety, Security, and Significance). Sometimes their complaints are with other people who have become substitutes, who they believe have let them down in some way. Rather than tell them to take responsibility for their actions, help them gain understanding of why they made these decisions in the first place, in the context of substitutes for loss.

If you are going through this book alone, ask God to help you understand the substitutes you have used to fill your loss in each area and identify whether they were real or phony substitutes.

To determine whether your substitutes have been phony or real, ask yourself these questions:

1. Is this substitute harmless, or has it enabled me to live a life that pleases God and does not violate Scripture? (To determine this, see whether it goes against Scripture.)

2. Is this substitute harmful or has it caused me to be unable to live a fruitful Christian life? (To determine this, see whether it goes against Scripture.)

Check which applies to each substitute.

- Substitute:

Harmless Substitute (Real) _____

Harmful Substitute (Phony)_____

Scripture Support

- Substitute:

Harmless Substitute (Real) _____

Harmful Substitute (Phony)_____

Scripture Support

- Substitute:

Harmless Substitute (Real) _____

Harmful Substitute (Phony)_____

Scripture Support

STEP THREE

Replacing the Substitutes with the Whole Truth and Nothing but the Truth

"Only fear the LORD, and serve him in truth with all your heart:
For consider how great things he hath done for you"
(1 Samuel 12:24).

Now that you have identified the loss and recognized the substitutes that have been used to fill the loss, it is time to replace the unhealthy substitutes with the whole truth and nothing but the truth. Listed below are the same categories of loss that you used to recognize the loss that has been experienced, but with some suggestions on how to begin the healing process by applying biblical thinking that will bring not only healing to the emotional wounds and difficult life issues, but will bring freedom.

When emotional wounds are created through any of these categories of loss, the individual finds that they are in bondage to situations they don't even understand. Lies have replaced the truth, and the only way to dispel lies is with the truth. Be willing to participate in your healing and to allow truth to enter into the dark areas of your life and shine light into what has been hidden. Now that you have identified whether your substitutes for your loss have been real or phony, use the following steps that apply to the categories of loss you have identified to guide you into your healing.

HOW TO RECEIVE HEALING BY USING THE NINE CATEGORIES OF SECONDARY LOSS

Category I
Loss Caused by Another's Sinful Choice
Reframed biblical thinking

"But if ye forgive not men their trespasses, neither will your Father forgive your trespasses" (Matthew 6:15).

1. Forgive (Matthew 18:21; Matthew 6:15). Pray and ask God's Holy Spirit to bring to your mind any people that you have not forgiven and after reading and meditating on the following verse of Scripture, list them and the circumstance below:

"Then came Peter to him, and said, Lord, how oft shall my brother sin against me, and I forgive him? till seven times?" (Matthew 18:21).

Pray: *I ask you Holy Spirit, to bring to my mind any people whom I have not forgiven and choose to be obedient to your Word and forgive them. I thank you Heavenly Father, that in Christ Jesus I am forgiven.*

- Lord, _____ has hurt me by:

It has caused me to:

I choose to forgive _____ for the hurt that was brought into my life, and how it made me feel.

- Lord, _____ has hurt me by:

It has caused me to:

I choose to forgive _____ for the hurt that was brought into my life, and how it made me feel

- Lord, _____ has hurt me by:

It has caused me to:

I choose to forgive _____ for the hurt that was brought into my life, and how it made me feel.

2. Pray and declare that no evil influence shall not have any hold on you. (You may want to list any evil influences that are brought to mind.)

"Thou shalt not bow down thyself to them, nor serve them: for I the LORD thy God *am* a jealous God, visiting the iniquity of the fathers upon the children unto the third and fourth *generation* of them that hate me" (Exodus 20:5).

- The following evil influences of another person's sin have affected my life in the following way(s):

3. Ask God to show you the substitutes for what was lost that you need to put off, and help you put on healthy biblical ways of looking at the loss. Your substitute may have seemed perfectly fine for a long time. Now you are realizing that it wasn't as harmless as you once thought it was. The Lord may be showing you, as you pray and consider His Word, that it was displeasing to Him.

"Every way of a man *is* right in his own eyes: but the LORD pondereth the hearts" (Proverbs 21:2).

- Unhealthy substitutes I have used:

- A new biblical way of dealing with this particular loss is:

4. Pray for your enemies (Matthew 5:44). <u>Don't skip this step.</u>

"But I say unto you, Love your enemies, bless them that curse you, do good to them that hate you, and pray for them which despitefully use you, and persecute you" (Matthew 5:44).

5. Press on. Determine in your heart that you will grow in maturity in Christ with enthusiasm, motivation, and with patience will run the race. Use this section to set your plan to press on and move ahead in your life. Include changes you need to make, old things that need to fall away, and new things that will help you to continue to walk in your emotional healing.

"Therefore leaving the principles of the doctrine of Christ, let us go on unto perfection; not laying again the foundation of repentance from dead works, and of faith toward God" (Hebrew 6:1).

- My plan to press on:

- Necessary changes I have to make:

- Old things that need to fall away:

- New things that I need to put on in my life:

When substitutes are discovered and can be identified with Category I—Loss Caused by Another's Sinful Choice, we need to reframe our thinking into the principles that Scripture gives us. Forgiveness is vital to healing from the loss caused by someone who hurt you, either with words, an action, or physical, or sexual abuse. Take the authority you have as a Christian, and in Christ, break off any evil influence in your life. Ask God to show you what substitutes need to be put off that were used to make up for the hurt you received. Also pray that the Lord will help you to put on healthy, biblical thinking to replace the unhealthy. Then pray for the salvation and sanctification of that person who hurt you. Resist any temptation to give up and persevere with confidence in your Christian life. Remind yourself that all your significance, safety, and security are in God your Savior.

Category II

Loss Caused by Your Own Sinful Choice
Reframed biblical thinking

"And ye shall know the truth, and the truth shall make you free" (John 8:32).

1. Ask God to reveal those sinful substitutes that must be removed from your life. Put on biblical thinking. List the sinful substitutes He brings to your mind, and dispel the lies with the truth.

- Sinful Substitute:

The Lie:

The Truth:

- Sinful Substitute:

The Lie:

The Truth:

2. God tells us to confess our sins and to repent (1 John 1:9; Luke 13:3; Psalm 32:1-2; Psalm 28:13). (Write down God's specific promises to you based on the following Scriptures.)

- "If we confess our sins, he is faithful and just to forgive us *our* sins, and to cleanse us from all unrighteousness" (1 John 1:9).

- "I tell you, Nay: but, except ye repent, ye shall all likewise perish" (Luke 13:3).

- "Blessed *is he whose* transgression *is* forgiven, *whose* sin *is* covered. Blessed *is* the man unto whom the LORD imputeth not iniquity, and in whose spirit *there is* no guile" (Psalm 32:1-2).

3. God will forgive us our sins. Read and meditate on the following verses and how they apply to you personally and write down what God reveals to you during this time.

- "For God so loved the world that he gave his only begotten Son, that whosoever believeth in him should not perish, but have everlasting life. For God sent not his Son into the world to condemn the world; but that the world through him might be saved" (John 3:16-17).

- "If we confess our sins, he is faithful and just to forgive us our sins, and to cleanse us from all unrighteousness" (1 John 1:9).

- "Giving thanks unto the Father, which hath made us meet to be partakers of the inheritance of the saints in light: Who hath delivered us from the power of darkness, and hath translated *us* into the kingdom of his dear Son: In whom we have redemption through his blood, *even* the forgiveness of sins" (Col. 1:12-14).

4. Choose to forgive yourself.

"Forbearing one another, and forgiving one another, if any man has a quarrel against any: even as Christ forgave you, so also do ye" (Colossians 3:13).

This verse includes you. Thank God, that in Christ you are forgiven. When you don't forgive yourself then you are saying that God's Word lies. If you don't forgive yourself, you are refusing the free gift of eternal life. Use this section to journal the freedom you receive when you accept Christ's forgiveness and stop rejecting the gift of forgiveness.

- The freedom I receive is:

5. Learn from your mistakes.

    When we have experienced loss from our own sinful choices in life, the loss often takes the form of consequences to sinful actions. Addictions can cause loss of relationships, or loss of health. The substitutes may be denial, blaming others, rationalization, or avoidance of close relationships. Sometimes they are overeating, drinking, or drugs. These things may be the substitutes for tav loss, or loss in the past before the addictions began.

    We all should learn from our mistakes. "Let a man examine himself" (1 Corinthians 11:28), is an invitation to consider the way we think. Exposing the lies from the way we were brought up and have responded to life's difficulties, is part of biblically restructuring the mind. Exposing the lies takes the power away from the lies so they can no longer hurt us. Our past responses to the peer pressure of ridicule may have caused bad choices.

The Lord Jesus was ridiculed, scorned, and sneered at, and did not respond. Hebrews 12:2-3 tells us how He handled the scorning. "Looking unto Jesus the author and finisher of *our* faith; who for the joy that was set before him endured the cross, despising the shame, and is set down at the right hand of the throne of God. For consider him that endured such contradiction of sinners against himself, lest ye be wearied and faint in your minds."

He despised the scorning, ridicule, and insults. The word "despising" means to de-esteem them by thinking against them. When you expose the lie of the sneer, you take its power or significance away, thereby protecting your own significance. You can't argue against ridicule. You can despise it, or de-esteem it, destroying its significance.

Category III

Loss from Living in a Sin-Cursed World
Reframed biblical thinking

"For the wages of sin is death, but the gift of God is eternal life in Christ Jesus our Lord" (Romans 6:23).

1. God promises a new heavens and a new earth.

"For as the new heavens and the new earth, which I will make, shall remain before me, saith the LORD, so shall your seed and your name remain" (Isaiah 66:22).

2. God promises to provide for our needs.

"But my God shall supply all your need according to his riches in glory by Christ Jesus" (Philippians 4:19).

We all have suffered loss from living in this world. It could be financial loss, or sickness, or a thousand other things. The danger for Christians is to blame others, or believe a non-Christian worldview, that the world is just, and benevolent, and major loss doesn't happen to good people. The truth is that we live in a sin-cursed, topsy-turvy world where good things can happen to bad people, and bad things can happen to good people. The promise for Christians is that God will turn the evil events for our good.

- What are some of the needs you are asking God to provide in your life?

Category IV

Voluntary Loss for Secondary Gain
Reframed biblical thinking

1. God promises us a future and a hope.

    "For I know the thoughts that I think toward you, says the LORD, thoughts of peace and not of evil, to give you a future and a hope" (Jeremiah 29:11, NKJV).

- What are the lies that you have believed about what God thinks about you?

- What is the truth about what God thinks about you?

2. God promises to give us the desires of our hearts.

"Delight thyself also in the LORD; and he shall give thee the desires of thine heart" (Psalm 37:4).

- The desires of my heart are:

3. Walk by faith and not by sight.

"For we walk by faith, not by sight" (2 Corinthians 5:7).

- In what area of your life have you been walking by sight and not by faith?

- How will walking by faith and not by sight in this area give you peace?

4. Keep your eyes on Jesus and the goal.

"Looking unto Jesus the author and finisher of *our* faith; who for the joy that was set before him endured the cross, despising the shame, and is set down at the right hand of the throne of God" (Hebrews 12:2)

Jeremiah 29:11-12, is always encouraging when we have suffered from loss. People who work and go to college, perhaps supporting a family at the same time, know this loss. They voluntarily put off the things that other people are getting to get the education, in order that they might be able to be better off financially later on, or reach their life's dream.

God does promise to give us the desire of our hearts if it is good for us and glorifies Him. It is especially important to strengthen one's faith when experiencing this type of loss. The enemy will say it is impossible, of no use, and discourage us if we let him. The means of getting a stronger faith is to do what God says: fellowship with believers, partake of the Lord's Supper, pray, read the Scriptures, serve others in your local church, hear the preaching of God's Word, use the spiritual gifts He has given you, such as tongues for edification, seek a prophetic word, or a word of knowledge from those who are gifted in the area of prophecy. Above all, keep your eyes on the Lord Jesus, and be patient. Eventually you will reach your goal. Don't give up!

Category V

Voluntary Loss for Christ
Reframed biblical thinking

"Yes indeed I also count all things loss for the excellence of the knowledge of Christ Jesus my Lord, for whom I have suffered the loss of all things, and count them as rubbish, that I may gain Christ" (Philippians 3:8).

Philippians 1:21; Philippians 3:7-8; John 12:24; Hebrews 11:24-27

1. Provision.

"But my God shall supply all your need according to His riches in glory by Christ Jesus" (Philippians 4:19).

2. Rewards in Heaven.

"Look to yourselves, that we lose not those things which we have wrought, but that we receive a full reward" (2 John 1:8)

3. God promises eternal life.

"That whosoever believeth in Him should not perish, but have eternal life" (John 3:15).

This brings to mind wives, or sometimes husbands, who have remained married over the years to spouses who have been unfaithful, because they want to be a good testimony, so that eventually the unbelieving spouse will come to Christ. It also describes people who have willingly put aside the benefits of living in the United States, to go and live in a third world nation, as a missionary, so that others can hear the gospel of Jesus Christ. Some have even laid down their lives for Jesus Christ. People like this have a definite call from God that enables them to remember that their rewards are in Heaven. This requires strong faith that patiently walks out the divine destiny. Although these people do not focus on the loss, they need encouragement from others. They need to be reminded that the Lord sees what they experience, and is pleased with them.

Category VI

Loss of a Loved One

Reframed biblical thinking

Matthew 5:4; 2 Corinthians 1:3-4; Isaiah 41:10; Isaiah 43:2; Psalm 18:28; Psalm 46:1-2; revelations 21:4; Psalm 119:50; Romans 8:18; 2 Corinthians 7:10; Psalm 18:2; 1 Thessalonians 4:13-18; 1 Peter 5:6-7; Psalm 23:4; Psalm 73:26; Psalm 22:24; Psalm 27:4-5; Psalm 30:5; Psalm 34:18; Matthew 11:28; Lamentations 31:33; Romans 8:31-39; 1 Corinthians 15:52-57; 1 Peter 1:3-9; John 14:1-4

- Life transcends death; no final separation from believing loved ones.

"Let not your heart be troubled; you believe in God, believe also in Me. In My Father's house are many mansions; if *it were* not *so*, I would have told you. I go to prepare a place for you. And if I go and prepare a place for you, I will come again and receive you to Myself; that where I am, *there* you may be also. And where I go you know, and the way you know" (John 14:1-3).

- There is the comfort of the Holy Spirit.

"And I will pray the Father, and he shall give you another Comforter, that he may abide with you forever; Even the Spirit of truth; whom the world cannot receive, because it seeth him not, neither knoweth him: but ye know him; for he dwelleth with you, and shall be in you. I will not leave you comfortless: I will come to you" (John 14:16-18).

- There is the comfort from the fellowship of believers.

"Paul and Timotheus, the servants of Jesus Christ, to all the saints in Christ Jesus which are at Philippi, with the bishops and deacons. Grace be unto you, and peace, from God our Father, and from the Lord Jesus Christ. I thank my God upon every remembrance of you, always in every prayer of mine for you all making request with joy. For your fellowship in the gospel from the first day until now; being confident of this very thing, that he which hath begun a good work in you will perform it until the day of Jesus Christ: even as it is meet for me to think this of you all, because I have you in my heart; inasmuch as both in my bonds, and in the defense and confirmation of the gospel, ye all are partakers of my grace. For God is my record, how greatly I long after you all in the bowels of Jesus Christ. And this I pray, that your love may abound yet more and more in knowledge and in all judgment; that ye may approve things that are excellent; that ye may be sincere and without offence till the day of Christ. Being filled with the fruits of righteousness, which are by Jesus Christ, unto the glory and praise of God" (Philippians 1:1-11).

- Time will help the grief.

"To everything there is a season, and a time to every purpose under the heaven: A time to be born, and a time to die; a time to plant, and a time to pluck up that which is planted; A time to kill, and a time to heal; a time to break down, and a time to build up; A time to weep, and a time to laugh; a time to mourn, and a time to dance; A time to cast away stones, and a time to gather stones together; a time to embrace, and a time to refrain from embracing; A time to get, and a time to lose; a time to keep, and a time to cast away; A time to rend, and a time to sew; a time to keep silence, and a time to speak; A time to love, and a time to hate; a time of war, and a time of peace" (Ecclesiastes 3:1-8).

Grief is something handled in an individual way. Not everyone responds exactly the same way according to the stages of grief that has been popularized. The stages do not follow one after another. Some are skipped over. Some never occur. This is important to remember because we all react differently and that is all right. For the believer, death is a temporary separation from a believing loved one. The Lord is touched by the feelings of our loss. The Holy Spirit will be your comforter at this time, reminding you of God's promises. Let others in to comfort you in their own way at this time.

The word people use called *closure*, is a misused term. When people are separated by death, our enemy, there is never *closure*. That person is always missed to some degree. Time will help us, by taking the rough edges off the pain of grief. That is a grace of God. However, the significance of that person in your life will never be forgotten.

Significance, safety, and security can all be lost when a loved one dies. Particularly when there was a good marriage where the couple loved one another, and each one built the other up, a loss of significance can occur. No one else will make that surviving individual feel as important as the spouse that died would make them feel. A woman, whose husband died, may now has to live alone. Safety is a loss that the woman feels, perhaps when she goes to bed at night. When the husband died, his pension stopped coming, most of his social security has ceased, and the wife, if he had no life insurance, has lost security. These three important factors of loss, on top of the normal grieving, put many risk factors for the surviving spouse to deal with, in terms of optimum mental health. The danger of depression is one possible problem that can arise.

So how do we heal ourselves from this category of loss? Remember that in God alone is your significance. You are important to Him. He gave His Son to die for you, a horrible death, that only He could accomplish for the complete forgiveness of your sins. The death of a person who belongs to Him is precious in His sight. The struggles and pain of the survivor who trusts in Him, is also precious to Him.

Even if no one else cares whether you live or die, God cares. He will not break the bruised reed, nor quench the smoking flax of faith. Your prayers are heard.

As far as safety goes, have faith in God. When there was no one to rescue the Israelites who stood waiting for the Pharaoh's army to slay them all by the seashore, God stepped in and opened up the Red Sea so they could escape. He will watch over you and assign His angels to take charge, so you can go to sleep in peace.

We are often tempted to torture ourselves over finances. How will I get along and make ends meet? God Himself is our security. Money may have wings, but God will provide for His people who trust in Him, even as the widow was told to gather the empty vessels and they were miraculously filled with oil.

Category VII

Loss Caused by the Actions of Another
Reframed biblical thinking

1 Peter 5:7; Romans 12:19; Luke 6:27-36

1. Trust in God to give you safety, security, and significance.

"Fear not, for I am with you: Be not dismayed, for I am your God. I will strengthen you, yes, I will help you. I will uphold you with My righteous right hand" (Is. 41:10).

2. Love one another

"A new commandment I give to you, that you love one another; as I have loved you, that you also love one another" (John 13:34).

3. Forgive

"For if you forgive men their trespasses, your heavenly Father will also forgive you." But if you do not forgive men their trespasses, neither will your Father forgive your trespasses" (Matthew 6:14-15).

"And be kind to one another, tenderhearted, forgiving one another, even as God in Christ forgave you" (Ephesians 4:32).

The very important truth, that God alone gives us true safety, security, and significance, is critical for believers to embrace with all their hearts, applying it in all their ways, and all their relationships, to have a healthy self-concept. Ideally, we should do this before we try to help someone else. Otherwise, we transfer our faulty, unbiblical thinking to them. In a related sense, the Lord Jesus warned people about Pharisees that were blind, leading others who were blind, into the pit.

As Jesus summed up the Law in the synoptic gospels by saying that we need to love God with everything we have, and to love our neighbor, as we love ourselves, we need the grace of God to even get close to doing that. Loving one another can mean praying for someone, and asking God to save that person.

Forgiveness is a concept that was borrowed by secular counseling from Christianity. Without knowing the forgiveness of the Lord ourselves, to do it their way will deteriorate into a cold neutrality at best. God commands His people to forgive with the warning that if we don't He will not forgive us our own sins (Matthew 6:15). Forgiveness can be done without having warm feelings for the person who has hurt us. It is an act of the will in obedience to God.

Category VIII

Loss Caused by Your Own Choice (Not Sinful)
Reframed biblical thinking

1 Thessalonians 4:6; Matthew 18:6; Ezekiel 33:6; 2 Corinthians 5:10; Psalm 25:1-22; Exodus 5:22-7:25

1. Realize that you are significant in God's eyes

"For You formed my inward parts. You covered me in my mother's womb. I will praise You, for I am fearfully and wonderfully made. Marvelous are Your works, and that my soul knows very well. My frame was not hidden from You, when I was made in secret, and skillfully wrought in the lowest parts of the earth. Your eyes saw my substance, being yet formed. And in Your book they all were written, the days fashioned for me, when as yet there were none of them" (Psalm 139:13-16).

"For God so loved the world, that He gave his only Son, that whoever believes in Him should not perish but have eternal life" (John 3:16).

2. Seek wisdom from God.

"If any of you lacks wisdom, let him ask of God, who gives to all liberally and without reproach, and it will be given to him…" (James 1:5).

3. Don't receive false guilt.

"It is for freedom that Christ has set us free. Stand firm, then, and do not let yourselves be burdened again by a yoke of slavery" (Galatians 5:1).

"Who will bring any charge against those whom God has chosen? It is God who justifies. Who then is the one who condemns? No one. Christ Jesus who died—more than that, who was raised to life—is at the right hand of God and is also interceding for us" (Romans 8:33-34).

4. Pray before you make future decisions.

"In all thy ways acknowledge him, and he shall direct thy paths" (Proverbs 3:6).

5. Move on because God has given you a future and a hope.

"For I know the thoughts that I think toward you, says the LORD, thoughts of peace and not of evil, to give you a future and a hope" (Jeremiah 29:11).

When people ridicule us, abuse us, and insult us, our self-concept may find itself agreeing with them on the inside. We then join in the abuse of others, and condemn ourselves, many times exaggerating our faults, and bringing down our significance in our own eyes. The real truth and just plain meanness blurs together and we can't sort it out accurately. This is the way we look at things from a natural point of view. This is not God's way. "Looking unto Jesus the author and finisher of our faith; who for the joy that was set before him endured the cross, despising the shame, and is set down at the right hand of the throne of God" (Hebrews 12:2).

What did Jesus do about the shame of contempt, mocking, and ridicule? He despised it. The word used in the New Testament means *to disesteem, to think against* (Strong's Concordance). In other words, pray and ask the Holy Spirit, who is our Teacher, to reveal the lie in the comment, to take the steam out of it, to disesteem it, to bring it down to what it is in truth, a lie, not to be received, to think against. Paul writes, "Casting down imaginations, and every high thing that exalteth itself against the knowledge of God, and bringing into captivity every thought to the obedience of Christ" (2 Corinthians 10:5).

James tells us to seek wisdom from God. "If any of you lack wisdom, let him ask of God, that giveth to all men liberally, and upbraideth not; and it shall be given him. But let him ask in faith, nothing wavering. For he that wavereth is like a wave of the sea driven with the wind and tossed. For let not that man think that he shall receive any thing of the Lord. A double minded man is unstable in all his way" (James 1:5). Notice that James connects seeking wisdom with living by faith. Biblical wisdom only works when faith is undergirding it. Wisdom is the practical application of knowledge, and with faith, can accomplish great things for God.

Category IX

Loss from Someone in Authority
Reframed biblical thinking

Luke 15:28: Story of the Prodigal Son

1. Realize that you are significant in God's eyes.

"For You formed my inward parts. You covered me in my mother's womb. I will praise You, for I am fearfully and wonderfully made. Marvelous are Your works, and that my soul knows very well. My frame was not hidden from You, when I was made in secret, and skillfully wrought in the lowest parts of the earth. Your eyes saw my substance, being yet formed. And in Your book they all were written, the days fashioned for me, when as yet there were none of them" (Psalm 139:13-16).

"For God so loved the world, that He gave his only Son, that whoever believes in Him should not perish but have eternal life" (John 3:16).

2. Seek wisdom from God.

"If any of you lacks wisdom, let him ask of God, who gives to all liberally and without reproach, and it will be given to him..." (James 1:5).

3. Don't receive false guilt.

"It is for freedom that Christ has set us free. Stand firm, then, and do not let yourselves be burdened again by a yoke of slavery" (Galatians 5:1).

"Who will bring any charge against those whom God has chosen? It is God who justifies. Who then is the one who condemns? No one. Christ Jesus who died—more than that, who was raised to life—is at the right hand of God and is also interceding for us" (Romans 8:33-34).

4. Pray before you make future decisions.

"In all thy ways acknowledge him, and he shall direct thy paths" (Proverbs 3:6).

5. Move on because God has given you a future and a hope.

"For I know the thoughts that I think toward you, says the LORD, thoughts of peace and not of evil, to give you a future and a hope" (Jeremiah 29:11)

When people ridicule us, abuse us, and insult us, our self-concept may find itself agreeing with them on the inside. We then join in the abuse of others, and condemn ourselves, many times exaggerating our faults, and bringing down our significance in our own eyes. The real truth and just plain meanness blurs together and we can't sort it out accurately. This is the way we look at things from a natural point of view. This is not God's way. "Looking unto Jesus the author and finisher of our faith; who for the joy that was set before him endured the cross, despising the shame, and is set down at the right hand of the throne of God" (Hebrews 12:2).

What did Jesus do about the shame of contempt, mocking, and ridicule? He despised it. The word used in the New Testament means *to disesteem, to think against* (Strong's Concordance). In other words, pray and ask the Holy Spirit, who is our Teacher, to reveal the lie in the comment, to take the steam out of it, to disesteem it, to bring it down to what it is in truth, a lie, not to be received, to think against. Paul writes, "Casting down imaginations, and every high thing that exalteth itself against the knowledge of God, and bringing into captivity every thought to the obedience of Christ" (2 Corinthians 10:5).

James tells us to seek wisdom from God. "If any of you lack wisdom, let him ask of God, that giveth to all men liberally, and upbraideth not; and it shall be given him. But let him ask in faith, nothing wavering. For he that wavereth is like a wave of the sea driven with the wind and tossed. For let not that man think that he shall receive any thing of the Lord. A double minded man is unstable in all his way" (James 1:5). Notice that James connects seeking wisdom with living by faith. Biblical wisdom only works when faith is undergirding it. Wisdom is the practical application of knowledge, and with faith, can accomplish great things for God.

STEP FOUR

Dealing with Future Loss God's Way
Reframed biblical thinking

"For to me to live is Christ, and to die is gain"
(Philippians 1:21).

There is an old expression that says *familiarity breeds contempt*. Some many times loss is spoken of in this book, but never get cavalier with the term, never let it become just a term. It is powerful, dangerous, and deeply destructive. It touches the emotional core like nothing else and can lead to the end of a life in God's image, or even the life of another. Cain experienced deep loss in his perception that too familiar story from Genesis. Looking back from our perspective, it seems much ado about nothing, leading to a crazy, needless murder. Looking at it from Cain's perspective it was nothing of the kind. It led to dark thoughts, a build-up of hidden volcanic emotions. When the tectonic plates of sin ground together in his inner person, it erupted in a rage that shook him to the core of his being, and left his brother dead and bloody on the ground. Take your losses seriously, because they have shaped your life to what it is now.

After dealing with your past losses God's way, hopefully, you are now in a position to begin dealing with future losses the way God has planned for you to understand them in His Word. The loss of significance, safety, and security can cause depression, and every other human condition that drives people to counselors. Knowing that the way we look at life comes from the way the people that raised us looked at life has given us a worldview that is uniquely our own. People that grew up in non-Christian homes, where the Word of God was unknown, developed in a way that handled loss in an unbiblical way. As you went through this book you have processed this and have renewed your mind God's way. This is amazing progress. As you are tempted to go back to the old way of handling loss, don't give in to the temptation that caused you to find an unbiblical substitute which created harm in your life. Be sensitive to the traps that were set for you in the past, and especially the triggers that made it seem so important to make decisions that later on decreased your significance, safety, and security. Remember that loss multiplies loss. Unbiblical thinking creates more unbiblical thinking, and begins to break the person down.

We are all different. Our losses are not always the same from one person to another. Only you know what would constitute a serious loss in your experience and situation. Make a list of possible losses that are particular to you and mainly the ones that would drive you to make decisions that would not please God.

Ask yourself how you would handle a possible loss in your life that affects your significance, your security, or your safety. Use your imagination, and then decide what you might have chosen for a substitute from your old way of looking at loss. Now ask God what He would have you understand about His nature that would reduce the pain and need for an ungodly substitute.

For example, God is our provider. Faith demands that we trust Him for the things that were taken away, whether it is a job, or a loved one. Our significance as a person may not be appreciated by others who have hurt us, but God has made us in His image, gave His Son for us, and values us. We who believe in Jesus Christ have significance in God's eyes.

The decision to cling to God may keep us from hoarding things in our loss. Money may be our loss, and we hurt because of it, but God is our security. He even sent an angel to provide for Hagar and her son when they had no more food in the wilderness and had no one to turn to. When God opened the eyes of the fearful people in Jerusalem to see the angels encamped around the enemy, it gave a sense of safety. God sends His ministering spirits to help us. We can't always see them, but they are there to help us, definitely with safety and security. Search the Scriptures and pray while you do it.

STEP FIVE

Loving Your Neighbor as Yourself
Reframed Biblical Thinking

Matthew 22:39; John 13:34-35; 1 John 3:17-18; Matthew 25:40; Galatians 6:9-10; 1 Thessalonians 5:11

God is the God of second chances. He forgives us and expects that we will forgive others. We all fail in doing this summary statement that Jesus commanded us to do in the gospels. Nevertheless, we hold to this as our goal to reach in this world, through God's grace. In applying this to ourselves and others, we can't love someone else if we can't love ourselves. One way of dealing with our hurts is to blame ourselves and beat ourselves up over it. Sometimes this may go on all of a person's life. You can't help someone else if you can't forgive yourself. Beyond the idea of forgiveness is another angle that needs to be discussed.

God may test us by putting someone in front of us to minister to when we are right in the middle of our own mess. Sometimes we may feel so sorry for ourselves that we don't want to hear about someone else's problems. An example of doing things the right way is Joseph in

Genesis 40. He is in the state prison of Egypt and finally got some authority, and now suddenly two big shots from Pharaoh's court are thrown into the prison. He is told to wait on them hand and foot. The amazing thing is that he does it with a good attitude. He doesn't tell them to get that glass of water yourself. Joseph does it all with a good attitude and even extends himself beyond his own problems to inquiring as to why the one man looks sad and uses the gift he had to interpret his dream. He could have said "Interpret it yourself." If he did that, he would have missed out on the greatest deliverance he could imagine, second in command to Pharaoh.

There will be times when helping someone else will seem too hard, but get out of yourself. If it wasn't too hard for Jesus to go to the cross for you, it shouldn't be too hard to show your gratefulness by giving out to someone in pain.

It is also very important that we realize that the person we want to help is different from ourselves. Why is this important? We may see some surface similarities, but each of our perceptions concerning our losses may be quite different. If we are to help someone else, and love them as ourselves, we would not want someone to think that they know all about our loss and come to the conclusion, that they could handle it, if it happened to them. This defeats us before we start getting help. Then we realize that that person did not understand us at all. This would never create a therapeutic atmosphere. We all have different perceptions of our losses and the quicker we accept this truth, the better off we are, as well as the person we are trying to help.

PART TWO
HEALING YOUR NEIGHBOR

STEP ONE
Helping Your Neighbor Identify Loss

"Look not every man on his own things, but every man also on the things of others" (Philippians 2:4).

The word neighbor is used because that is how the Lord Jesus describes those whom God places in our paths so we can love them as ourselves and thus fulfill the Law of God, Jesus' way. Christian counseling is not some oddity to help people. It is the heart of ministry to suffering people who are hurting from the fall-out of sin. It is simply Christianity in action with a precision that has been needed for a long time. Presuming that you are reading this book as a people-helper, you are privileged to have in your possession a means of getting past the symptoms and reaching the complicated depths of the problems that ruin relations, and cause untold pain in the minds and lives of people. Paraklasis Counseling Theory (PCT), is the tool that God has given to us to bring healing in a new way to honor the Father, the Son, and the Holy Spirit and His Word.

Before people can change, they need to understand the cause of the problems in their lives. So far as has been discerned, loss is the cause of all emotional distress and pain in the minds of people. After initially hearing the presenting problems of the person who you are trying to help, give them The Nine Categories of Secondary Loss, and assist them in helping them to discover which category of loss is at the heart of the problem.

You can't change anyone, and they will not change unless they want to change. They need hope and that comes from the promises of God, prayer, and the power of the Holy Spirit. As someone who has been placed by God in a personal relationship with people who want help, it is the people-helper's responsibility to instill hope, encouragement, and comfort as the Paraklatos, the Holy Spirit does in our lives. "But the Comforter, which is the Holy Ghost, whom the Father will send in my name, he shall teach you all things, and bring all things to your remembrance, whatsoever I have said unto you" (John 14:26). As a counselor to people, you are like the Holy Spirit, called to their side, to be one who teaches, exhorts, intercedes in prayer, helps them, and leads them to a deeper knowledge of the Word of God, seeking God to give them divine strength to undergo the trials of this life.

When the Holy Spirit teaches us, we begin to see and understand the things in our lives that are both good and bad, strengths and weaknesses, as well as understanding the loss and its effects that has come our way. As counselors we need to help the person to see the loss and to trace its path into the life. Let them have a copy of the nine categories of secondary loss and pray with them to ask the Holy Spirit to give them light.

The category of loss they choose is probably not something in the present, although it could be, and may, on the surface, not seemingly be related to the presenting problem. Loss needs to be replaced with something, and that substitute may be the presenting problem.

STEP TWO

Helping Your Neighbor Identify Substitutes, Phony or Real

"...that you put off, concerning your former conduct, the old man which grows corrupt according to the deceitful lusts, and be renewed in the spirit of your mind, ²⁴ and that you put on the new man which was created according to God, in true righteousness and holiness" (Ephesians 4:22-24).

"Depart from evil and do good; seek peace and pursue it" (Psalm 34:14).

"I beseech you therefore, brethren, by the mercies of God, that you present your bodies a living sacrifice, holy, acceptable to God, *which is* your reasonable service. And do not be conformed to this world, but be transformed by the renewing of your mind, that you may prove what *is* that good and acceptable and perfect will of God" (Romans 12:1-13).

When you did this for yourself, you discovered that God helped you to identify these substitutes for the loss in your life. The ones that harm you are the phony ones and the ones that were God's choices helped you. For example, a mother who lost her son in the war started a support group for widows. This helped her in her loss, and was not a harmful substitute. An individual who lost his house from a now become active in her spare time with the Mothers' Against Drunk Drivers organization. John Walsh, the host of the television show, America's Most Wanted, originally got involved in criminal investigation on a global level after his own child, Adam, was kidnapped and found decapitated. What a terrible loss and trauma, so he chose a direction in life that would help others in that type of loss, Category One, Loss Caused by Another's Sinful Choice. These are examples of good substitutes for the deep hurt from loss in a person's life, but there are more harmful ones.

The depression may be the presenting problem, but the substitute may be causing the depression because the person may realize that the substitute is wrong, and may feel guilty about it. The substitute may be cutting, which satisfies, at least partly, because the person feels something, even if it is pain. The loss may be in the past, when the person lost a loved one and has not dealt with it God's way. That loss may have come through death, divorce, or rejection.

The goal is to help your neighbor see for themselves the unbiblical choice they made, repent of it, and begin to understand the original loss from God's point of view. When that happens, the cutting will stop.

As a counselor, you are concerned to help your neighbor to identify the harmful substitutes in their lives that have created the pain they are presently suffering. The person you are trying to help must come to the place where they recognize the connection. It is not enough that you see it. Simply giving them knowledge of it is not going to change anything. The person being helped must grasp it on a deeper level than just information, so that there are emotional feelings involved, and a motivation for change that comes from the inside, not the outside.

STEP THREE

Helping Your Neighbor to Replace the Phony Substitutes with the Whole Truth and Nothing but the Truth

John 8:32; Ephesians 6:14; Romans 12:2; Numbers 23:19; 1 John 1:9; 1 Timothy 2:5

When the word *phony* is used to describe substitutes, it means that which is harmful, sinful, and not God's way of dealing with loss. The word *phony* sometimes describes people that present their character as good, when in reality, it is bad, usually to bring misfortune to the person that is being deceived. Another term describing a phony is a con-man.

In the spiritual world of demons and angels, demons are the ultimate phonies. They lie and offer solutions to the loss that people suffer. The Bible describes demons as lying-spirits.

(2 Chronicles 18:21) "And he said, I will go out, and be a lying spirit in the mouth of all his prophets. And the LORD said, Thou shalt

entice him, and thou shalt also prevail: go out, and do even so." God is not the only one who can speak. It is so important that when you are feeling a traumatic loss in your life, and are at your weakest point, you compare the voices you hear with what the Bible teaches, and if it is not what the Bible teaches then it is not from God. Do not receive that suggestion, reject it in Jesus' Name. That is how the devil makes inroads into a person's life to choose phony substitutes that will finally bring only pain, misery, and despair. The substitutes that are demonically suggested are evil and it is sin to do them. They are phony in that they offer what appears to be a sensible solution to a painful loss, and like the con-man, will swindle you out of your peace, relationships, and anything good.

What about people going through a crisis? You might be called upon to come over and help with a family crisis from a frantic neighbor. Here is an example. A car of teenagers are going home on the last day of high school when the new driver loses control and drives into a deep pond on the curve of the road. As the car sinks, the boy driving is able to get out of his seat belt but is unable to get his girl friend and his sister out of their seat belts. He swims to the surface and they drown. You answer your phone later in the day and you are asked to come over to the home where the surviving brother lives. This is upsetting. You have no clue as to what you are getting into or how people will respond to you, whether you will be welcomed or not.

A crisis is a time of trouble where even worse outcomes are possible and the uncertain outcome feeds the emotions and unravels a person's sense of control, making a crisis worse in terms of perception. Sometimes a person's perception is even worse than the crisis itself. It is important to gain an understanding of the person's perception of the crisis in their thinking. Ask yourself whether significance, safety, or security is being threatened by the loss. Maybe, as in the above example, all three are threatened. The surviving brother could be suicidal. The parents may be blaming each other for the sister's death and letting the son, who is a new driver, take the car to school. The death of a child puts tremendous strain on a marriage. In this case, the marriage was already in trouble, and when you get there, you discover that the father is on the premises, but won't come into the house. You must go out and talk to him and first find out if he is suicidal. Then go in and talk to the mother, looking into suicidal ideation as well.

Tension and stress are running high at this house, as is the case in any crisis. As these increase, normal skills for coping are overwhelmed, grow weaker, and can become ineffective. Good family resources consist of effective communication, flexibility, and cohesion. As a result of the tragedy, these characteristics do not work well in this particular family and they are in real crisis.

The book of Philippians consists of powerful examples in handling stress and tension to deal with a family crisis. The book is addressed to the church family as Paul considers them brothers. If the family can reframe the stressors, then the outcome would be positive. "Be careful for nothing; but in everything by prayer and supplication with thanksgiving let your requests be made known unto God" (Philippians 4:6).

The word "careful" means anxious. All resources for dealing with stress originate from God by giving grace through the supply of the indwelling Holy Spirit (1:19), or changing the circumstances and bringing about safety. In the case of the traumatic death of the sister, and the family perhaps not even Christian, you must pray and ask God for grace and for Him to intervene, protecting the lives that are so damaged from getting worse. At the present time, showing support, checking for danger to themselves or others, and trying to get some sense of control for the family to operate in is the most important thing. Other suggestions that are described are for later counseling. At this point, they may be in shock, pretty much unable even to grieve much. In this situation, significance, safety, and security have been diminished, and their lack of effective communication, family cohesion, and flexibility creates a crisis of magnum proportions.

This particular crisis situation is placed here to let you know that not all who invite you to counsel them are going to be easy. It will take time. The problem for counselors is often hoping they will come back. If they do, then is the time to apply principles of Scripture to help them to reframe their harmful thinking into biblical principles to deal with the loss in a God-honoring way.

Substitutes for loss are not always clear. In the above scenario, there clearly is a tragic loss, for more than one family. The father may have lost a sense of significance within the marriage, even before the loss of the daughter. He could have lost even more significance by self-blame, which would be Category VIII, Loss Caused by Your Own Choice. Perhaps he thought that it was his fault because he let a new driver, his son, take the car on a dangerous road. Loss multiplies loss and the human mind has a distorted sense of justice, in which the loss must be replaced by an equal substitute. Since the father would not enter his home, it is a clue that he could be in serious danger of suicide. The equality demanded by that serious loss is a life for a life. The substitute would be suicide. This is a phony. It is a distortion of justice. This is where the good news of the gospel is the answer if the man is open to it. Any loss that we have caused, no matter how much justice demands equality in a substitute, justice was already met on the cross, by Jesus' atoning death. The same kind of equality by suicide as a substitute for the loss of the sister may be the brother's problem. His also is a loss of significance and Category VIII secondary loss is applicable. The mother may be suffering from a loss of security, and be in despair. She may be losing her husband, her financial security, her daughter, and possibly the son. Suicide may be a possible substitute for all the loss she perceives. This is how the PCT counselor has to think in order to be of help to those who are hurting.

Suicide is a terrible thing that hurts all those who were close to the person who killed themselves. Ministers who have done funerals for those who committed suicide will agree that there is such a black atmosphere around the visitation at the funeral home and also at the service at graveside. It is a selfish act that leaves children wondering if they will wind up doing the same thing some day. Anyone who is trying to help hurting people needs to keep a watchful eye on the client concerning this possible action.

Confronting a suicidal decision is the counselor's responsibility. Being sensitive and listening, the paraklasis counselor will recognize the rigid, negative view of self by acknowledging the depth of the feelings and then attempt to replace the loss of significance, security, or safety, with true biblical significance in a warm, empathic atmosphere. If there is a spiritual willingness then a biblical reframing of the trigger event can proceed. If there is no interest in spiritual things then the 3 Ss (safety, security, significance) must be found in something else.

PCT is broadly applicable to crisis situations. It can reach the objective of changing people through Jesus Christ by attainable goals which include replacing the maladaptive substitutes for safety, security, and significance, since these three basic needs of man will be found in God alone. Primary loss can be met in receiving God's invitation through the Gospel for restoration of relationship with Him. Secondary loss in whatever category can be restored to true safety, security, and significance found in Scripture by replacing poor substitutes.

No one likes to feel like a failure or a nobody. Sometimes suicide seems like the only way out, the only solution. Loss from the past, or even the perception of loss in the present or future lies in the thinking of the person committing suicide.

Some people believe that they have significance, but it may be a false significance. False significance leads to little significance. Little significance leads to no significance. Here is an example. Ecclesiastes 2:9-11 tells us that the king is great in his own eyes because he can enjoy all the pleasures of the world. He rejoices in his worldly occupation. After all, he is the king at the top. Eventually, his satisfaction diminishes, and does not satisfy. This is when the substitutes begin to fail. This loss of significance is like a cancer that leads to less and less significance, before being eaten away. (v.11)...*all is vanity*. Eventually it led to ...*hating life* (verse 17), which means no significance. Loss multiplies loss. Loss itself begins with the earliest age of a child. When the child is born, there is the loss of leaving the comfort and quiet environment of the womb. Perhaps this is why babies cry when they are born. This integration of a loss experience into the functioning of a person right from the beginning of their life creates the potential for personal growth or deterioration. When substitutes fail, deterioration can lead to suicide. When it reaches suicide we can speak of total loss.

An example may be a top Hollywood actor who has fame, fortune and is one of the top comedians in the world. He has found substitutes for primary loss. They seem to work. Suddenly it is all over the news. He has committed suicide. It shocks everyone. He seemed so happy, to have everything. Whatever the loss, the substitutes began to fail him. Finally, the only partner willing to dance the idolatrous dance of life was death. A person may be symptom free yet have the same invisible substitutes for primary or secondary loss. In total loss that brings one to suicide, people are like the king in Ecclesiastes 2:17, *hating life*. We can never neglect the spiritual component in counseling.

STEP FOUR

Helping Your Neighbor Deal with Future Loss, God's Way

Philippians 4:6-7; Psalm 121:1-8; Isaiah 40:28-31; Matthew 6:6; Matthew 21:21;
James 5:16; Psalm 100:1-5; 2 Corinthians 4:8-9; Psalm 91:1-3; Proverbs 15:22;

We have discussed helping our neighbor who wants help, how to discover the loss, find the substitutes and then help them reframe their thinking according to scriptural principles. How does the one who is being helped view future loss? How will they deal with it? When safety, security, and significance is threatened, will they jump backwards and find the same old substitutes and put them on, like old shoes? This is something that those you help must consider.

If the person is helped, then as a counselor you must do everything that you can do to assist the one you helped to maintain their freedom.

No one knows the future but God. We never know what losses we will experience in this world. That is why it is so important to be able to identify that loss and put it in a category to understand it. None of us when facing a loss should be muddled in our emotional feelings so we are confused and can make bad decisions. Identifying the loss from the nine categories does not make that loss go away, but it is the beginning of moving forward so the loss does not result in harmful substitutes. Prevention, as is said, is worth a pound of cure.

Once the loss is identified, steps need to be taken to make sure that the loss is handled God's way. "A bruised reed shall he not break, and the smoking flax shall he not quench: he shall bring forth judgment unto truth" (Isaiah 42:3). It is God's desire that we all learn the principles in His Word so that the wind of God's breath will blow upon our faith and not allow it to be put out by the trials of life that we all experience.

Safety when acquired must be rooted in Christ, and the claims of God which is in His Word. "Wherefore ye shall do my statutes, and keep my judgments, and do them; and ye shall dwell in the land in safety. And the land shall yield her fruit, and ye shall eat your fill, and dwell therein in safety" (Leviticus 25:18-19). In order to prevent a repetition of seeking unbiblical substitutes for loss incurred in the future, the first thing that must be done is to live a life that seeks to please God by obedience to the Bible. The above passage shows that safety can be rested in, if we do God's statutes, keep His judgments, and do them, or obey God. This is conditional.

The Scriptural context for the idea of security includes much that is relevant for the PCT counselor. All of the phobias are fears. Fear produces anxiety and depression. Man's shelter and preservation does not come from the limited security of the things of this world, but in the attributes, character, and transcendent promises of God. "For thou hast been a shelter for me, and a strong tower from the enemy" (Psalm 61:3). Security is about confidence. Our confidence is based on past experiences with God; how He helped us, or how He directed our steps and provided for us. This builds up our faith. David had many close calls in his running from Saul, but God did miracles to deliver him out of them all. He had hope because he knew that God was his strong tower. God was his shelter. Our security rests in Him. The person we are helping should grab hold of Scripture to face the troubles loss brings in the future. Our security will always be in Him.

It is tempting to use the secular term self-esteem for the word significance. Self-esteem has to do with self-importance, a term foreign to what pleases God. The word significance implies the work of God within a person. The significant person has meaning in life because of his humility, wisdom, and boldness. This grows out of his relationship with God on a daily basis. The Apostle Paul had significance not from being a Pharisee, for he counted that as loss in comparison to his salvation in Christ and knowing Him. God turns loss on its head from a biblical perspective. Christ gives us confidence in the present and a sure hope for the future. Our meaning for living is because we belong to Jesus, our being made in the image of God, and being adopted into God's family, based on the forgiveness of our sins because of Jesus' work on the cross. When future loss threatens our significance, remember that God has significance and because we are made in His image, we ought to have it as well.

Job in his troubles still shows healthy significance in that significance is expressed by the fact that God was his hope and strength. "Finally, my brethren, be strong in the Lord, and in the power of his might. Put on the whole armour of God, that ye may be able to stand against the wiles of the devil" (Job 6:10-11).

It is not pride, but an awareness of self-identity in relationship to God which governs relationships with man. A healthy significance keeps one from pride and is more related to humility. Again, significance comes from God. The Lord Jesus is our example (John 8:54). He is not concerned with honoring Himself, but finds His significance from God. True significance places all of life under God's ownership (Acts 20:24) as the Apostle Paul puts his coming death in its proper place, under the call of his life. A healthy significance is also expressed in a conscious desire to avoid offence to God and man (Acts 24:16). To possess a biblical sense of significance is to reflect in life the servant heart that we see in Jesus and shown by the Apostle Paul. "For though I be free from all men, yet have I made myself servant unto all, that I might gain the more" (1Corinthians 9:19).

Paul keeps his hand on the plow, looking forward, like a runner, looking forward to the finish line. Significance involves looking forward with hope for the future. (Philippians 3:13-14) "Brethren, I count not myself to have apprehended: but this one thing I do, forgetting those things which are behind, and reaching forth unto those things which are before, I press toward the mark for the prize of the high calling of God in Christ Jesus." The above descriptions of a true biblical significance show that it is not just inward, but has practical purposes in serving God, as love is expressed to our neighbor.

"Nor of men sought we glory, neither of you, nor yet of others, when we might have been burdensome, as the apostles of Christ. But we were gentle among you, even as a nurse cherisheth her children" (1 Thessalonians 2:7). We don't have to strive for our significance in life. Rather to reframe it biblically, let God raise us up, and be gentle, not allowing an angry defensiveness be our attitude, but be a servant.

"There are, it may be, so many kinds of voices in the world, and none of them is without signification. Therefore, if I know not the meaning of the voice, I shall be unto him that speaketh, a barbarian, and he that speaketh shall be a barbarian unto me" (1Corinthians14:10-11). The word for importance, or the idea of significance is from the Greek word "dunamis," or power. It is the same word for the power that raised Jesus from the dead. A lack of significance is meaninglessness, or being voiceless. No one will listen to you. Significance means having meaning in life, being important enough that you have a voice.

STEP FIVE

Helping your Neighbor Love his Neighbor as Himself

1 John 4:20-21; 1 Corinthians 13:1-3; 1 John 4:11; James 1:27; Hebrews 13:16; John 3:17; Philippians 2:4; Matthews 25:35-40; James 2:14-17; Proverbs 19:17; Luke 3:10-11; Acts 20:25-28; Romans 15:1; Galatians 6:2

One of the greatest ways to help someone is not so much to help him with his problems, but to get him past looking at himself, and staring at his navel. Some people who go for counseling pride themselves on learning some psychological jargon. They continue to go on getting counseling, always focusing on them, and never learning to care about others. God does not want Christian narcissistic people, but people who are interested in being a blessing to others. When this is inculcated, the person will not be focused on his problems, but looking outward to be about God's business. In other words, he becomes less selfish.

An example would be Joseph, whose story comprises the last twenty one chapters of the Book of Genesis. After Joseph went through incredible loss, loss of family, freedom, friends, and reputation, he learns to forgive and love those brothers that initiated his terrible experiences. "Then Joseph could not refrain himself before all them that stood by him; and he cried, cause every man to go out from me. And there stood no man with him, while Joseph made himself known unto his brethren. And he wept aloud: and the Egyptians and the house of Pharaoh heard. And Joseph said unto his brethren, I *am* Joseph; doth my father yet live? And his brethren could not answer him; for they were troubled at his presence. And Joseph said unto his brethren, come near to me, I pray you. And they came near. And he said, I *am* Joseph your brother, whom ye sold into Egypt. Now therefore be not grieved, nor angry with yourselves, that ye sold me hither: for God did send me before you to preserve life. For these two years *hath* the famine *been* in the land: and yet *there are* five years, in the which *there shall* neither *be* earing nor harvest. And God sent me before you to preserve you a posterity in the earth, and to save your lives by a great deliverance. So now *it was* not you *that* sent me hither, but God: and he hath made me a father to Pharaoh, and lord of all his house, and a ruler throughout all the land of Egypt. Haste ye, and go up to my father, and say unto him, Thus saith thy son Joseph, God hath made me lord of all Egypt: come down unto me, tarry not: And thou shalt dwell in the land of Goshen, and thou shalt be near unto me, thou, and thy children, and thy children's children, and thy flocks, and thy herds, and all that thou hast And there will I nourish thee; for yet *there are* five years of famine; lest thou, and thy household, and all that thou hast, come to poverty. And, behold, your eyes see, and the eyes of my brother Benjamin, that *it is* my mouth that speaketh unto you. And ye shall tell my father of all my glory in Egypt, and of all that ye have seen; and ye shall haste and bring down my father hither. And he fell upon his brother Benjamin's neck, and wept; and Benjamin wept upon his neck. Moreover, he kissed all his brethren, and wept upon them: and after that his brethren talked with him" (Genesis 45:1-16).

Evidence that Joseph forgave his brothers was that the first thing he did was to send everyone out of the room so he could talk privately with them. He did not want their dark past and guilt to be exposed. If he wanted to, he could have had them all killed, but he did not have that inner attitude of unhealthy bitterness. Nevertheless, forgiveness is a conscious choice Joseph had to make toward his family. What helped Joseph was reaching out toward his brothers when he saw the pain of their own consciences condemning them that was expressed on their faces, as they must have felt that judgment had finally come for their sin in Dothan, so long ago.

The surest sign that someone you try to help is getting better is when they begin to care about others. This is what is seen in the story of Joseph. Instead of angry words for what they had done to him, Joseph lifts the guilt and pain, from them, whether they believed it or not, by telling them that there was someone other than them that turned around that awful situation to save their lives and their families' lives as well as the whole surrounding world.

Helping others to not continually feel sorry for themselves is a step in real healing. "Look not every man on his own things, but every man also on the things of others" (Philippians 2:4). The Apostle Paul drives home the reason for caring about others in the context of the next section. The grounds for doing this is to have the mind of Christ. We are to look at others the way He did. We are to treat others the way He did. It involves sacrifice, and a dying to self and all that would come naturally to say and to do. That is what we see in Joseph, and that is what someone who helps another to help another should be doing. This is modeling that the helper does to help someone help someone else.

As Christ is the image of the Father, we are the image of God, and our lives should model the example of Jesus our Savior, whose image we are becoming. And this is on the inside as well as the outside. Modeling is not done in a cavalier fashion, but with prayer and personal soul-searching before God. Taking the mind of Christ is a step of great humility that is willing to help others, even if it costs us something.

Seeing God's good hand on your life is the key to loving your neighbor as yourself. If you accept God's plan for you even if you do not understand it, you won't tend to be jealous over what God is doing for someone else. The greatest thrill of being a Christian is the blessing that thrills your heart when you minister to someone in the Name of Jesus.

Using your spiritual gifts for others is something that makes you care about others. Giving, encouraging, teaching, praying, bringing hope, or salvation, or healing, or deliverance to someone makes us smile, as it does God. "…Thou shalt love the Lord thy God with all thy heart, and with all thy soul, and with all thy mind. This is the first and great commandment. And the second is like unto it, Thou shalt love thy neighbor as thyself. On these two commandments hang all the law and the prophets" (Matthew 22:38-40).

RECEIVING AND GIVING WISE COUNSEL

Ps. 16:7 - "I will bless the Lord who has counseled me"

Ps. 73:24 - "With Thy counsel Thou wilt guide me"

Prov. 11:14; 24:6 - "in abundance of counselors there is victory"

Prov. 12:15 - "a wise man is he who listens to counsel"

Prov. 19:20,21 - "listen to counsel and accept discipline..."

Isa. 9:6 - "His name will be called wonderful Counselor..."

Jn. 14:16 - "I will ask the Father, and He will give you another Helper"

Jn. 14:26 - "the Helper, the Holy Spirit, will teach you all things"

Jn. 15:26 - "When the Helper comes, He will bear witness of Me"

Jn. 16:7 - "the Helper,...I will send Him to you"

Rom. 12:8 - "he who exhorts, in His exhortation"

Rom. 15:4 - "through the encouragement of the Scriptures, we might have hope""

Rom. 15:14 - "able also to admonish one another"

2 Cor. 1:4 - "able to comfort those who are in any affliction"

Gal. 6:1 - "you who are spiritual, restore such a one in a spirit of gentleness"

Col. 1:28 - "admonishing every man and teaching every man with all wisdom..."

1 Thess. 5:11 - "encourage one another, and build up one another"

1 Thess. 5:14 - "admonish the unruly, encourage the fainthearted..."

Heb. 3:13 - "encourage one another day after day"

Heb. 10:25 - "encouraging one another"

SCRIPTURE SUPPORT FOR HELPING YOUR NEIGHBOR

Mark 12:31 – "And the second [is] like, [namely] this, Thou shalt love thy neighbour as thyself. There is none other commandment greater than these."

Leviticus 19:18 – "Thou shalt not avenge, nor bear any grudge against the children of thy people, but thou shalt love thy neighbour as thyself: I [am] the LORD."

Luke 6:27 – "But I say unto you which hear, Love your enemies, do good to them which hate you…"

Matthew 22:36-40 – "Master, which [is] the great commandment in the law?"

Romans 13:8-10 – "Owe no man anything, but to love one another: for he that loveth another hath fulfilled the law."

Matthew 7:12 – "Therefore all things whatsoever ye would that men should do to you, do ye even so to them: for this is the law and the prophets."

Luke 10:25-37 – "And, behold, a certain lawyer stood up, and tempted him, saying, Master, what shall I do to inherit eternal life?"

1 John 4:16 – "And we have known and believed the love that God hath to us. God is love; and he that dwelleth in love dwelleth in God, and God in him."

Romans 15:2 – "Let every one of us please [his] neighbour for [his] good to edification."

Matthew 19:19 – "Honour thy father and [thy] mother: and, Thou shalt love thy neighbour as thyself."

John 15:12 – "This is my commandment, That ye love one another, as I have loved you."

Matthew 7:1-2 – "Judge not, that ye be not judged."

Colossians 3:12-14 – "Put on therefore, as the elect of God, holy and beloved, bowels of mercies, kindness, humbleness of mind, meekness, longsuffering…"

Matthew 18:15-17 – "Moreover if thy brother shall trespass against thee, go and tell him his fault between thee and him alone: if he shall hear thee, thou hast gained thy brother."

1 John 4:21 – "And this commandment have we from him, That he who loveth God love his brother also."

ADDENDUM

What makes a self-help book better than another? There are many good books on the Christian market that truly help people. One quality about this book, that sets it apart from many others, is its broad research base. That information is found in the prior book, *Paraklasis Counseling Theory*, which is a Christian approach bringing healing to universal loss, shows the validity of the new Christian counseling theory, describes it, and includes all the research done supporting it. Twenty-three pages of bibliography reflect that research material. *Heal Yourself Then Heal Your Neighbor*, which is a five-step approach to emotional healing, putting that theory into practical application.

Undergirding Paraklasis Counseling Theory (PCT) is its biblical foundation. Numerous examples are given showing the different categories of loss in the Bible. It has a solid theological foundation as well. It has a Trinitarian structure and is based on the Father, Son, and Holy Spirit. Through this book you will see a threesome structure that derives from the Trinity. For example, significance, safety, and security are found in our relationship to God and the three persons of the Trinity. Various triads are found in the Bible.

Thanks to research that showed a need for a universal model of loss, it gave some added insight into the development of PCT. Studies in Terror Management Theory, including how people react when they are threatened with death, what happens to their worldview, and their various behaviors, have all contributed to PCT thinking and development. Other research has shown high reliability and validation for the idea that Christians have, in general, a better response to stress in life than the unbeliever. One research article made the clear distinction between just church-goers, and those who had an internalized belief system, in other words, knew Jesus Christ as their Lord and Savior. The saved were able to be stronger in the face of death, and had better all-around mental health, than the people who may have externally been religious, but not internally.

One thought that has come out of PCT is that loss multiplies loss. When loss occurs, there is a tendency to find a substitute for that loss. Sometimes the substitute is harmful and creates problems of its own, so in that sense, loss multiplies loss. At the same time, healing multiplies healing. As Christians, our blessings are other people's blessings. That is why this book has the added component of helping your neighbor. So, healing multiplies healing.

Every area that we have examined that people come to counseling for can be traced back to loss in some form or another. This has been demonstrated in people who are in crisis and are traumatized. Another example are people who are suffering from PTSD. They have suffered terrible loss, particularly veterans. In a time of increased domestic violence, with physically and sexually abused children, there is also a loss of significance, safety, and security, since those that should have been trusted, couldn't be trusted.

The homeless population have great loss which is the problem behind much of their emotional suffering and partly the cause of their being homeless to begin with. Education is not an insulator against loss. Many homeless people are highly educated. There is a lack of security, safety, and significance that comes from loss. Again, loss multiplies loss.

Younger women who have had high levels of stress early on in their marriage, double the chances of getting Major Depressive Disorder in later life. This came from loss of the 3Ss. The stress of couples who lose a child to death, puts tremendous strain on the marriage, and many do not make it. Whether families are suffering, or people suffer through body image problems, loss is at the root of it all.

This is why PCT is the answer to primary and secondary loss in the lives of Christians and non-Christians. Counseling is a war, but thanks be to God that He gave His Son to insure that the war can be won. The hope for all of us as we help ourselves and others is that the Holy Spirit, who knows the depths of the suffering, and what to do about it, helps us to see the blessings of helping others.

CONCLUSION

Loss is so universal that we all tend to take it for granted, especially when it happens to someone else. This book is not a mechanical step-by-step list of changes for a person to do and then everything magically gets better. PCT involves the hearts and emotions of the counselor and the counselee. Jesus shed tears (John 6:35). He can be touched by the feelings of our infirmities. As people helpers, let's not forget to be human and connect with the people we are trying to help. Speak the truth in love. Truth comes first, and don't let your emotions make you compromise God's Word.

Sin is ugly, harmful, poisonous, and contagious. At bottom, we are contending against a spiritual serial killer. Exposing loss, and discovering the substitutes that have met the devil's approval and have caused so much destruction in a person's life is what the PCT counselor is truly about, in other words—about the Father's business. If we remember these warnings and encouragements there is not a more joyous, and more celebrative, satisfying activity to do than to help somebody in distress.

A further suggestion for anyone who has enjoyed reading this book, and was helped in their efforts to help people, is to get the book that this book is based upon, *Paraklasis Counseling Theory, A Christian Approach to Healing Universal Loss.* This will give you a deeper understanding of how PCT is the first Christian counseling theory. It will elaborate on how it is biblically and theologically based, and will provide the scientific research that undergirds the theory. In addition, it gives many biblical examples of loss of significance, security, and safety, as well as how it applies to crisis counseling, children who have been sexually, physically, and verbally abused, ministering to the elderly, the homeless, and many other areas of counseling. It is a great resource book for people helpers.

We both want to thank you for purchasing this book and we pray that you will be blessed as you set yourself free and help your neighbor as well. We believe you will be motivated in your counseling to—more than anything else to—**GIVE GOD THE GLORY!**

Made in the USA
Columbia, SC
25 June 2021